Lean Analytics

The Ultimate Beginner's Guide to Build a Lean Startup using Data

Anthony O'Brien

Table of Contents

Introduction

There is this burning desire to create, to build something out of nothing, to give life to ideas that lie deep within us. The Entrepreneurial mind strives to grow ideas into successful business enterprises. However, building companies out of ground-breaking ideas is not an easy task. Rather, it is one that requires effort and a lot of hard work.

For the Entrepreneurial mind like you and I, we are resolved to putting in the work, pulling up with grit and advancing our ideas with determination.

In all truth, building anything takes time. Whether it's your dream house or a global business, the factor of time is critical and indispensable. However, the estimated time to achieving these goals can be shortened considerably by certain tools. If you're building a house, a concrete-mixer would save you a lot of time and effort.

What if I want to start a business? Is there a tool like this for me? You may ask. This book contains a detailed answer to your question; the summarized answer to this question budding in your heart is visible in the title of this book, LEAN ANALYTICS.

Lean Analytics is an arm of the Lean Start-up model (a method used to greatly shorten product creation and development cycles and determine the viability of a proposed model or product).

The Lean Start-up has three stages to its product development cycle: Build, Measure and Learn. This methodology stresses on efficiency in the smallest possible time. This is the key to an effective product development cycle.

Entrepreneurs, Companies and businesses alike are expected, in creating a new product, to firstly create and develop (build) a product we call the MVP (Minimum Viable Product) and then 'put in the hands of your consumer' to measure how effective this product is (how much of a solution it is to consumer needs, the level of satisfaction derived from it, its faults) and then taking this data (learn) and using it to improve your product, continuing this cycle until you reach the desired 'perfect' product.

The Lean Start-up has been adopted by many companies, tech giants and businesses. This is because it doesn't just reduce the risk of mass-producing products that are not viable in the market; it also gives a real-life evaluation of your product, giving you the chance to fine-tune it till it solves the consumer problem it was created to solve. The fine-tuning is done by simply iterating an existing product.

As evident from the Cycle, data is a very important aspect of the Lean Start-up and this is where Lean Analytics comes in. Lean Analytics is the measure and learn part of Lean Start-up. It is using data to create better products that are viable in the consumer market. A Lean Entrepreneur or company needs to measure so it can be able to learn. It also needs to know what things to learn, the importance of getting this data (the why), and the right approach in obtaining this date (the how).

However, the lean process is not only restricted to the confines of product development. Lean in a more wholesome outlook is all about maximizing consumer satisfaction, employee interaction, engagement and profit.

Lean Manufacturing, Lean Start-up, Lean thinking, Lean management, and Lean principles are some of the methodologies that can help you create a lean organization. Although this book is focused on Lean analytics (a part of Lean start-up) we shall examine all of these methods in different aspects of business.

In this E-book, we will discuss some important aspects of lean analytics and how to deploy lean. We will go into the intricacies of lean in the workplace, how to implement it in management and running of the business, how to use lean in service management. This book is not limited only to entrepreneurs or businesses, we will discuss how to use lean in the public sector too. When you are done with this book and you get to the last page, you would have been equipped with all that is needed to employ lean analytics.

Creating a new product can be a very risky endeavor, a possible hit or miss, but with the right tools, processes, and techniques at your disposal, it has the possibility of being a strike. Knowing how to deploy lean analytics ensures you give you consumers 'what they want'.

It's my desire that when you read this book, you see the pros of using lean analytics and adapt it to your business; in production, consumer relationship, Human resource management, and other aspects of your business.

Introduction to Six Sigma

What is Six Sigma?

If you've heard about Lean Methodology, then you'd find it easy to understand Six Sigma. The six sigma is a set of methodologies and tools used for the improvement of the procedure. This method was first introduced by Bill Smith, an American engineer who worked at Motorola in the year 1980. The six sigma process requires that at least a percentage of over ninety-nine digits of the probabilities for producing a particular aspect or feature of a part must be proven to be without defects.

The aim of the six sigma process is to provide improvement to the quality and value of the result of a procedure through the identification and elimination of those items responsible for defects. On the other hand, also, it seeks to reduce the diversities in the procedures of business and production. In order to achieve this, six sigma makes use of some set of methods effective for managing quality. These methods are mostly verifiable by experience and observation and statistical. Six

Sigma makes sure it creates a unique set of persons in the company or organization that are trained as professionals in using these methods.

Every six sigma project has a laid out chronology of steps which it follows in an organization. Each of these projects and methods have a quality target. The targets defer, and the target could be in view of increasing profits, it could be to provide satisfaction for the customer, it could be to eliminate the cost of production, it could be to cut down on pollution or to reduce the time of process cycle.

The six sigma methods calculate progress through ascertaining how much defects a certain method was able to help eliminate.

The six sigma method is somewhat like Lean, and they can both comfortably work hand in hand. Lean runs on a number one priority of satisfying its customers whichever way, and that also could apply to Six Sigma; it aims at satisfying its customers through creating and delivering high-quality products.

Six sigma operates on a set of principles, and one of the main principles it operates on is first identifying the need of the customer. Mostly, the customer's need either has to do with the time of delivery, the cost of the products, or the quality of the product, especially as regards faults and malfunctions.

Once the need of the customer is established, development becomes effective immediately towards providing a solution to meeting the customer's need. These needs are categorized by their differences — for example, cycle time, and defect rate. Then a performance target is set for the purpose of meeting the need at hand and the professional persons equipped with the sigma methods set to work.

Just like most of Lean's methods, six sigma is repetitive and is based on a high level of discipline in adopting the processes. The six Sigma principle aims at the development and delivery of near excellent products and services, and that is to be done with consistency.

The six sigma principle is ensconced on the concept of statistics; these measures progress as it has to do with faults. It is used to identify a deviation in the process of production. The six sigma, as earlier stated, is continuous, especially if a method proves effective; it is continued for the sake of the improvement it brings.

One major reason why it is a continuous process is seen in the fact that it provides a structured method for businesses with which they can measure and analyze their progress, help them reveal how they are performing at the moment as well as how they can improve on their performance in order to get the result that is required of them, effectively and efficiently. It helps increase their productivity in a continuous process.

How does Six Sigma work?

The six sigma problem-solving method makes use of a framework known as the DMAIC framework. DMAIC is a representation of five phases of the problem-solving technique.

These five phases or stages are:

- Define

- Measure

- Analyze

- Improve and,

- Control.

Each of these steps helps to streamline and highlight a business process in order to discover problems and invent solutions to them.

Define: in this phase, a project and its process are presented, and data is collected. An outline of the aim of the project will be made, and a kind of blueprint is set. Information such as the business idea, a statement of the problem, a statement of the goals and objectives, the region or scope of the project, the resources, a graphical representation of the process events as it is meant to occur, and an estimate of gains. All of these make up the defining level in a six sigma project.

Measure: after defining the project, the next stage that follows is the measuring stage. Here, the variables in the procedure are measured via the collection of process data first. The baseline will be acquired, while the metrics will be compared side by side with the metrics of the final performance. Then, the ability of the process will be determined and procured.

Analyze: under this stage, a root cause analysis is carried out, where complex and certain tools effective for analysis are utilized and applied in order to find out the root cause of a fault in a project. Some of such tools and equipment used to determine these problem causes are the Pareto charts and histograms; even fishbone diagrams are used.

On the other hand, also, hypothetical tests are carried out in order to verify and validate these root problem causes such as ANOVA tests; ANOVA is an acronym for analysis of variance and Regression tests.

Improve: Prototyping, stimulation study, and designing of experiments, these are steps that are taken towards improving on the problems discovered under the analysis stage and eradicating these root causes. The moment these final root causes are discovered, what follows is the formation of solutions for the improvement of the process.

Control: A control system is a system following the improvement stage, after the implementation of solutions for the derived problem, how much the solution was able to achieve has to be recorded and documented. What a control system does is that it helps to monitor or check the performance of the process after it has been improved.

If a solution fails, a plan known as the response plan is created to take care of and manage the failure of the solution. The procedure is usually standardized through the use of a control plan and project instructions. These are what make up the control stage.

A control chart is designed for the purpose of representing the performance of the process. Control charts show the process performance. The benefit and gains of the project are talked on, and they are verified against the estimate. Generally, the purpose of this stage is to ensure that the benefits are held together.

Remember that the main focus of any six sigma project is to cut down on the faults and defects of a project and manage variations. In order to achieve this, a whole lot of mental exercise will have to go on. Outside the box pattern of thinking and the ability to be innovative is highly required. There are two possibilities at hand; one is the need to improve on an already existing and working process, while the other is developing a completely new workable process altogether. The latter can be as a result of no process at all, or the presence of a very terrible process. If the process is not good, then it is equal to no process at all.

It is to this effect that the DMAIC framework is applied. A six sigma project must boast of meeting the needs aimed at by a six sigma methodology. When a project requires an entirely new Six sigma method, the implication is referred to as a Design For Six Sigma (DFSS), and that requires what is known as an (IDOV), an acronym that represents Identification, Designing, Optimization, and Validation. Usually, a project may require a whole new process because, in order to achieve the level of improvement required, a whole new process has to be adopted.

Certain factors are usually put into consideration, such as the competition, and the design has to do with gathering as many possible solutions as can come up with, and pick out the best of them.

The project or rather process performance is optimized through the use of a set of statistical and advanced branding and replicating methods as well as the polishing of patterns. Before any design is validated, however, it must be in accordance with the goals of the process.

In the excitement of applying the six sigma method to your business or project, it is very expedient to have in mind the fact that what size sigma is about is not just increasing the quality of a product, but rather, it is interested in improving the quality of a product to satisfy the customer. What that simply means is that if tampering with the product does not in any way satisfy or impress the customer, then there really is no need for it. Some businesses fold up because they fail to realize that their customer has to like what they are given. The improvement is so that the customer is satisfied, so the improvement should be one that the customer requests for.

This goes ahead to explain that the customer is the number one defining factor of what improvement you will make in your product.

Improving the product you offer is good, but assessing what the actual need of your customer is, is way more important than improving the product. Your customer may love just what you offer. Think of all the companies and businesses you know that wrapped it up at some point even though they started out very well. Probably they even folded up while furnishing their product and producing even way better products. Polaroid is an example of such companies. And to think that they actually adopted the six sigma methodology.

Just like Lean Methodology, six sigma has gone way beyond just reducing defects to reducing cost and on to creating more value. The six sigma is not interested in anything more than pleasing, appealing to, and satisfying the customer. This also helps you tower above your competition. The six sigma, just like Lean again, promotes excellence, provided it is excellent in the eyes of your customer.

The Six Sigma Tools

In order to carry out the steps in the five main DMAIC stages earlier mentioned, those who adopt the Six sigma methods make use of certain tools. Below are the tools used by six sigma project users:

- Pareto Charts

- Design of Experiments (DOE)

- Analysis of Variance (ANOVA)

- Regression Analysis

- Failure Mode and Effects Analysis (PFMEA)

- Fishbone Diagrams

- Time Series Plots

- Hypothesis Testing

- Histograms

- Applicability of Six Sigma

Primarily, the six sigma methodology was developed for the process of manufacturing. Other than that, however, the methods and techniques can still be adopted by and applied by many other companies and industries around the world, provided that they are intelligent enough to apply some modifications where and when necessary.

Six Sigma can work for a software development organization that uses DMAIC for the purpose of prioritizing the upgrade of products and also to cut down on the cost of customer service.

The six sigma concept can be applied in any industry, it doesn't matter the quantity or quality with which you deal, the concept is that of constant and iterative improvement, and it is not very complex. The six sigma can be applied in the aspect of time management, it can apply in the aspect of improving a product, and it can also be applied in the aspect of reducing coats and eliminating defects.

The 1.5 Sigma Shift

This is a theory in the six sigma method that, over time, a process will most likely shift from the target it has been set for by about 1.5 worth of sigma value. The permission for this to happen gives birth to the overall accepted six sigma value, which is 3.4 defects per million opportunities.

When this is ignored, that is, the 1.5 sigma shift, it gives birth to a six sigma value, which is of 2 defects per billion opportunities. However, the ideal objective for processability is 3.4 defects per million, and this means an almost zero-defect process and very numerically negligible. Statistically, nonetheless, a six sigma process implies two defects per billion opportunities. You might wonder how a 2 per billion opportunities suddenly transforms to 3.4 per million opportunities, and that is where the 1.5 sigma shift comes in.

In using the six sigma methodology, expectations should not be ruled as absolute. While the six sigma is expected to yield a certain result, the 1.5 sigma shift provides a variation possibility in the long run. Having this possibility in mind will rather equip you to prepare for adjustments. A process should never be expected never to alter once it begins. There is always a need for improvement, and if intact, the process works, that is a sign that more can and should be done.

This is the idea behind or rather the math of the 1.5 sigma shift. Remember that six sigma is a statistic project management method. Think of an objective that has to be achieved within a given surrounding and certain conditions applicable to that surrounding. If you will make any plan or set any objective, you have to think of two possibilities.

Imagine that plan being executed under a standard or excellent condition, or imagine swapping to a different condition that may bring about a variation. Now, no matter how fixed a process maybe, over a period of extended time, the surrounding elements or condition will eventually change, and this is what brings about variations. That being the case, right from the moment of planning, the changes that will occur has to be provided for through creating a balance. The balance would be something that can create an adjustment or makes up for the change when it occurs. This will enable the long term objective is still achieved. That unavoidable change is the 1.5 sigma shift.

How to utilize Lean

In the past 20 years and even more recently, a lot of companies and businesses in various industries have displayed a greater interest in discovering and exploring how to use the lean start-up methodology for running their businesses. Lean, to the person hearing it for the first time, might seem a bit unclear, rooted in a modern perspective on the workflow strategy instead of a practical and daily style which can be established in a generalized way so that everyone who works in your company, organization or business can relate and flow with. The reality with the lean method is that, with this style of management, once you go deeper, you would find out that the lean method transforms how business is run and handled.

Lean's benefits go a long way beyond the success of the project and revenue growth. You see, companies, startups, and businesses that have used lean start-up methodologies have been known to gain successes and profits in various aspects of business. Such gains include better team management, increased team morale, efficient business processes and so on. Successful lean management often results in an overall efficiency in business administration and management.

However, the gains with lean are often the unexpected value that is derived when these strategies are used. For example, Lean practices are focused on limiting or reducing the workflow such that less is used to produce more. However, something that typically happens is that the customer experience significantly gets better with each iterative product in the lean cycle. This helps the reputation of your business.

In turbulent and crisis times, it is appropriate to re-examine all the processes and functions of the organization to assess their effectiveness, efficiency, cost-effectiveness, and ethics. This chapter focuses on a function of particular relevance, but to which so far less importance has been given: lean procurement process. Procurement is the set of processes for the initiation, planning, development, acquisition, and logistics of goods and services for the organization. Unlike the simple supply chain, it also includes strategic and external aspects of the organization. Procurement must be considered a function of the organization's line since acting on significant costs contributes substantially to the margins.

To achieve a lean workflow, there are several tools that can be used. Popular concepts range from the extraction system just described to strategy tests, A / B tests, minimum value product tests and a variety of other valuable tools. There is no single trick to implement Lean, but by using the information obtained from the survey data gotten from the Lean Business Report on knowledge work, there are three tools used more often when you want to go lean in business management.

This chapter deals with procurement from the point of view of lean thinking and Six Sigma, lean thinking, whose goal is to increase value for the customer and for the organization through integration and elimination of waste. The method is referred to as lean procurement. The topic is tackled in its entirety by examining all aspects of procurement management, from organizational aspects to the support of IT systems, from the point of view of documentation to that of collaboration with suppliers. The method is referred to as lean procurement. The topic is tackled in its entirety by examining all aspects of procurement management, from organizational aspects to the support of IT systems, from the point of view of documentation to that of collaboration with suppliers. Method aspects are integrated with many examples of practical applications that can be considered best practices in the application of lean procurement in organization through integration and elimination of waste. The method is referred to as lean procurement. The topic is tackled in its entirety by examining all aspects of procurement management, from organizational aspects to the support of IT systems, from the point of view of documentation to that of collaboration with suppliers. Method aspects are integrated with many examples of practical applications that can be considered best practices in the application of lean procurement. from the point of view of documentation to that of collaboration with suppliers. Method aspects are integrated with many examples of practical applications that can be considered best practices in the application of lean procurement. From the point of view of documentation to that of collaboration with suppliers, method aspects are integrated with many examples of practical applications that can be considered best practices in the application of lean procurement.

The Seven Steps to Lean Implementation:

Initial System Assessment

1. Assess if the company is prepared for the cultural change that will come

Who will be the project leader?

We need to find a leader for the project and this person must be able to draw up a plan, articulate that plan and resilience to execute the plan even under adverse pressures.

In addition, an external consultant, with experience and competence is needed to guide the leader through the difficult times and questions he will go through. This is one of the best investments you can make.

Do we have organization improvement specialists to make this endeavor a success?

Are there people with good training in improvement tools and skills?

Do they have the ability to analyze data and processes? If this group is not ready yet, what is the training plan? The sensei will be fundamental in this assessment.

2. Evaluate the present state of the production system

Evaluate if the steering is compromised.

For this type of initiative is not enough to get involved, it is necessary commitment! Evaluate if the processes are ready for the initiative.

These four pillars should be at a minimum at the stage defined below, otherwise develop a plan to reach them and include it in your schedule.

Stability (absence of special causes) and quality (little variation): At least all critical features are identified and most feature stability and meet quality requirements.

Machine downtime: downtime is known and less than 2%. Team prepared for continuous improvement: There is a team prepared with the ability to carry out highly complex improvement projects.

Continuous Improvement Philosophy: Projects are carried out regularly and top management is involved in these initiatives.

Standardization techniques: policies and methods are documented; problems recur after a long period and break.

3. Assess the need for workforce training and perform the necessary training.

Introduce the subject to senior management in an 8-hour training session about Lean's house. These people need to understand Lean house concepts and experience variation reduction, Tact time calculation, OEE and line balancing simulations.

Do a 4-hour training with all the people in the factory. Group them up to 50 people and pass the concepts of line balancing and continuous improvement to everyone. These people should be able to perform Kaizen in their activities.

Execute the training plan for the specialized personnel that will be the soul of your project.

These people should be able to structure improvement initiatives, guide and conduct the necessary information gathering, and develop, test, and implement all opportunities discovered.

Introduce the topic to senior management in an 8-hour training session about Lean's house. These people need to understand the concepts of Lean's house and experience it. These people should be able to structure improvement initiatives, guide and conduct the necessary information gathering, and develop, test, and implement all opportunities discovered.

4. Document the present state of the value stream

Prepare a VSM of the current state. Document the value stream, the current lead time, inventories, setup time.

5. Redesign system to reduce waste

Synchronize supply with customer demand.

Meet customer demand and prepare your line to produce on time.

Synchronize production.

Balance your line and production steps according to time and create streams Try to minimize the wait time.

Calculate lead time and try to reduce it. Try to eliminate all activities that do not add value. Create pull systems.

Have a fixed maximum inventory according to customer demand and safety stocks.

Activate production only when parts of your fixed inventory are consumed by the later step.

6. Evaluate and determine the goals for the line.

Determine the critical indicators for the line. Determine the goals for each indicator so this drives everyone's behaviour.

It is useful to view indicators on a trend or control chart.

Whenever the indicator does not meet the targets, prepare an action plan - be sure to consider the causes of variation present!

7. After the changes, evaluate the new current state, stress the system and return to step

The process of making a lean factory is the pursuit of continuous improvement. As we improve one part of the system, others appear as opportunities. Stressing the system serves to highlight problems that were hidden (by waste) and thus achieve an even better level of performance.

This is a cultural change that every organization should seek.

As you saw above, the Lean Manufacturing methodology can be implemented through 7 STEPS.

Now that you know this, you can fulfill the role of a strategic and operational leader within your company regardless of the corporation's business segment.

How to analyze your Workforce through Lean

The concept of workforce analysis (known in English as Workforce planning), is not a very recent concept, however, it is not a well-known concept in the world of small or medium-sized businesses since the management and management of their Workforce is usually not very complex. However, this concept has been gaining importance among large corporations that have a global presence and have been forced to think and manage their human capital in a much more strategic way within an increasingly competitive market.

The concept of workforce planning can be understood from its simplest way, such as planning the number of employees and staff that are needed to carry out an operation of an organization in an appropriate manner, to the more complex approach that provides a strategic approach and global to not only ensure that you have the necessary staff, but to know where to have it, when to have it, how to obtain it and how to evolve it in a way that represents a competitive advantage for a complex organization.

The concept of workforce Analysis

There are numerous ways of describing workforce analysis in its simplest form workforce analysis; "the strategic planning of the workforce serves as a managerial reference framework to make decisions regarding staffing to have the right number of people with the right set of skills in positions and times adequate."

Together with this, it is vital to note an important factor for many companies, and it is the cost factor; In this way, it is not only knowing when, how, where and the characteristics of the workforce, but knowing how to include the cost factor to create an adequate balance and allow the company to be competitive.

The concept, therefore, is a complex concept, which is not based solely on one dimension (quality, efficiency, effectiveness, cost, etc.) but on the combination of all these dimensions, so that they serve as a frame of reference to make the most convenient decisions according to market conditions, the mission of the company and the objectives and goals of each of its business units that collaborate in achieving the overall goal of the organization.

Based on the above, this concept should, therefore, be conceived as a tool of great value for any global company in achieving its strategy as a business, and not only as a responsibility of the human resources department but as a network of decisions between the operational, the tactical and the strategic.

We observed in our study of workforce analysis that something that is extremely crucial and is the concept of temporality. Workforce analyzes should show trends, which indicates that nothing is static 'conditions change and therefore, the strategy must adapt to present conditions and prepare for future conditions.

If one takes into account a current situation, without considering the past (as a certain phenomenon has evolved) and the uncertainty of the future, very possibly the decisions taken are not the right ones. In the same way, if only one dimension related to the workforce is analyzed, without taking into account multiple dimensions (geography, job family, job level, performance ratings, tenure, business unit, etc.) and compare them with the objectives of the company to achieve a much more holistic and efficient analysis.

Each organization should be alert about the condition of its workforce and business needs, as well as the demand for skills and knowledge and of course the availability (local or global existence) of people with that knowledge or skills required.

A very important concept is "headcount" (known by the acronym HC in many companies) and that it is used as a basis for doing workforce analysis, where the budget dictates the "headcount", based on cost Average of an employee and what can be paid for a particular period.

The purely cost-based approach, neglects aspect as crucial as the need to have the right human resources to comply with the business strategy, and as may point out the problem with pure financial analyzes is that they may not distinguish between people who represent only a cost to the company and those who are actually an investment; that is, those who add value through research and development of products, services, and relationships with customers and consumers and even those who add intangible value through motivation and commitment that general in the workforce.

It is, therefore, this, a critical point that we wish to highlight in this reflection; not conceiving workforce planning as a mere financial exercise of cost per head because it is in that approach that the principle and value of workforce planning are lost. There are many other dimensions that should always be considered, including the "know-how" that is often lost when reducing staff in an organization or moving operations to other countries.

May shares a very interesting picture of the factors that should be taken into account when working on workforce planning.

As a summary, there are 5 critical factors that must be rescued:

- The vision and the strategy
- Demographic changes
- Technological change
- The capabilities that are needed
- The supply of both internal and external talent

Vision and strategy are crucial to define the structure, qualities, qualities, and location of the workforce. If the workforce does not align with the company's strategy, the entire planning exercise has no value.

Demographic changes cause an important impact on the analysis of the present and future workforce.

Through the proper analysis of these changes it can be determined how the organization can obtain advantages from the new profiles of potential workers (for example: more technological, with greater knowledge and specialization in certain fields, with the management of one or more languages, with a capacity of leadership and communication different traditional approaches, etc.) and design the strategy to also allow the integration of current and future generations with the experienced workforce that has been in the company for several years and even for decades (to facilitate the gap generational in work environments).

The change in information and communication technologies directly affects the company's ability to automate processes and make them much more efficient, reduce the need for certain positions that do not generate value and develop staff to take on greater challenges within the company and organization taking advantage of its experience and knowledge while allowing it to evolve and create more added value.

The capacities that are needed are always linked to the needs and evolution of the market. And because the global world is increasingly demanding, every organization must be aware of changes in demand, which at the same time influence the need for a workforce that adapts to these changes and facilitates the achievement of a clear competitiveness over other companies.

These capacities can vary from technological knowledge, the ability to research and develop new products and services, to other skills related to the ability to work in collaborative virtual teams, rather than traditional hierarchical models.

The provision of trained people is extremely important since it is what allows organizations to direct their attention to certain geographical locations where they can more easily get personnel that have these critical skills and not run the risk of reaching a point where they lose Competitiveness for not having the right staff to achieve your goals.

Importance of Workforce Analytics:

This is definitely an aspect that summarizes the importance of workforce planning. This process allows the organization to anticipate changes, creating a bridge between what you have in the present and the vision of what you want to have in the future, within the general vision and goals of the company.

An effective workforce planning process goes beyond a few discussions about what the organization will need in the future, but that it consists of creating a blueprint of how it will be acquired, adopted and adapted to achieve the workforce that the company needs.

In summary, workforce planning is of paramount importance for any company, not only those large corporations, but any company, regardless of size, since the concept itself allows the organization to anticipate and act, not in a manner reactive, but proactive, anticipating needs and preparing to cover them.

As you might have noted, workforce planning is much more complex than one might think.

If the organization understands the structure, composition, skills, and abilities of its workforce, it can design an action plan to make the necessary adjustments that allow a difference between an average performance and be a leader in the market in which it operates.

What Lean thinking can do for Entrepreneurs

Entrepreneurship is a strong word that has found its way into the business and enterprise environment. This word has fought, to receive the recognition it now has in the visions and missions of various business organizations. But unfortunately, when this term is used, it is usually to depict small-scale ownership management.

On a broader view, however, to understand the concept of entrepreneurship, the Lean Thinking framework can be employed. But before we consider how and the extent at which Lean Thinking affects entrepreneurship management, it is apposite to understand what Lean Thinking is all about.

Lean Thinking:

You might have heard of Lean Management, which has its origins dated back to the 80s during Toyota's revolution of the manufacturing world. Of course, after the revolution, certain things were put in place to favor entrepreneurship management.

Lean is a flow – a series of positive flows. It is a mind-set set on removing anything that challenges the satisfaction and comfort of the customer. In other word words, lean is embarking on activities that provide optimum customer value while also bent on eliminating any activity that does not portray this vision.

People often consider Lean as making money. Well, every business aims to generate revenue. The purpose of Lean, as we will see in the case of entrepreneurs, is to ensure that values are supplied to the customer. This is through products designed to cater to the needs of the customers.

This waste management thinking has helped a lot of businesses shape their visions in creating substantial products with value-filled services and not just producing to make money. Of course, income will flow in as a result of massive sales. It is a beneficial situation both for the manufacturer and the customer.

The customer enjoys the product; the manufacturer receives his pay.

So, lean thinking is just not some other word. Many business owners have employed it. Whether to execute an idea for a start-up business, although it has a minimal effect or to increase the fortune of an already established enterprise.

All You Need To Know About Lean Thinking:

By now, you should know that Lean thinking involves waste thinking management. That is, thinking the right way and channeling your efforts into satisfying your customers by producing value-added products. Below is what you need to know about Lean thinking.

More Than Just Cutting Cost:

Lean is not reducing the cost of production. Rather, it is finding a balance between affordable products and the satisfaction to be derived from them. Even if you want to cut costs, at least make the benefits worth the money. In general, lean involves making plans to create a product with values the customer will be interested in enjoying.

Step-By-Step:

You are expected to have a clue as to what you are going to be making. A business plan must be launched first by a hypothesis. In this way, you can see similar products in the market, how they are distributed, and the rate at which they are consumed. Testing hypothesis gives you the understanding of your proposed product, whether it is a marketable product or otherwise. If there is, the product is then tagged as a Minimum Viable Product. In essence, lean thinking involves starting with a hypothesis and not just launching the business immediately.

Learn What People Want:

Calling the workforce into a corner of your company would not solve the problem of what people want or how you can satisfy them. You need to learn by doing some research. All plans must be made upfront, so it is important to have the necessary information before production.

Lean thinking helps you have real-time experience with the customers, and you can build the product in line with their taste and expectations.

Get Ready To Run:

You cannot always be in the same position. "No Growth" is terrible for business. Big enterprises, including start-up businesses, are sure to have ups and downs at one point in time. There will be discouragement, break in production, and other hazards surround the business world. So, to thrive, get ready for the bad times.

When a situation goes south, one of the most effective ways to quickly overcome it is by overturning it into an opportunity. But how can you do this if you do not have a standby plan? In other words, make plans to change the product on the run and have a strong team that can thrive in such a situation.

Consider the critical lean formula on facing uncertainties: "chaos + speed + pivots = success."

Find Your Network:

When you have studied the market place, structured out your business plan, and have started making waves, find out others like you. Another best idea of lean thinking is that it gives you the avenue of looking at what similar producers are doing wrong to help you improve your products.

Are There Principles?

Yes, there are. Founders of the Lean Enterprise Institute, James P. Womack and Daniel T. Jones, first described the five known principles of lean in 1997. We are going to consider these fundamental principles.

Find the Value:

The first application of lean involves identifying the values derived from the product. This involves taking a study of the use of the product by the customer, to know what kind of value or benefit is attached to the product. This way, you can prevent waste, set a reasonable target price, and ensure that the price is proportionate to the value attached.

Some most common questions asked here include; what is the need of our customers? What do we produce to satisfy this need?

Check the Value Stream:

This requires knowing the steps, procedures, and materials for the production of the product. To cut down cost and prevent waste, you must identify and remove those processes, resources, or other things attached to the production which do not add any value. You must ask these questions as regards checking the value stream; where and how fast can we get the materials? Where and how do week keep our tools?

Make the Flow:

When you have identified those things that do not add value and have discarded them, next is to create new steps. This principle directs that you must ensure that you create a value-filled production chain, maximizing efficiency, and avoiding waste. The principle of creating an effective flow ensures that the production processes fall in line with each other and that there is no delay. Questions that can pop up, in this case, include; will start work early get the job done faster? Is there a way we can bring in more machines? How do we get the products to the customer more quickly?

Establish Pull:

When does the customer need the product? And how do we quickly respond to the order? These questions help you to make ready all necessary chains of production so that there is a fast response to the customer's request.

Find Perfection:

In conclusion, lean helps you identify areas that need improvement. Those who follow these principles are somewhat called "perfectionists" because they look for nothing short of perfection. At every point in time, they evaluate every process to increase value.

In summary, the Lean principles work hand in hand, and as stated, they follow the cycle. So, you must make sure one does not affect the other.

What Lean Thinking Can Do For Entrepreneurs

Do not ask if there is there any assurance that lean thinking will help businesses in this modern day. Instead, consider the fails you will encounter if you do not subscribe to a Lean methodology. It is not a get-things-done-quick model; it is a long term process that assures continuous improvement.

Higher Level of Productivity:

Applying Lean thinking helps you identify values, eliminate procedures that do not add values, and ensure efficiency.

Fast and Smooth Operations:

After you have eliminated the non-value adding processes, there will be more focus on ensuring the streamlined processes flow smoothly. There will be a quick response to the customer's order, and the production cycle will flow as expected.

Quality Products:

Because you regularly evaluate the production processes, you can identify and approach quality issues with ready problem-solving tools.

Assured Customer Satisfaction:

This is a major aim of Lean. To provide value to the customer and satisfy them. By adequately managing waste thinking and processes, you will be better equipped with functional tools to help meet the demand of the customer.

Use of Resources:

With lean, you know when to produce and how to produce. This way, you prevent waste. When you consider the demand before you produce, you will only use as many resources as needed.

Rework:

Lean eliminates rework, which costs time, resources, and money. Having to deal with defects may cause you to lose the customer.

Efficient Workforce and Work Environment:

Because you have streamlined the processes to only value-adding ones, there is an active, skilled, and competent workforce. Also, the environment will be conducive, as there would not be unnecessary tools or processes running.

Greater Level of Responsiveness:

Your operations will be flexible, and you will be better able to respond to orders when the customer pulls. Like "Just In Time" manufacturing, lean will help you get the product the customer needs and get it ready when it is required.

Increases Everything Else:

When you begin to enjoy the benefits of lean in the above-listed ways, it also improves everything else. Meaning, when all these happen, there are more orders, more on-time productions, more sales, more deliveries, and more money. In all, lean is the best option if you want to grow your business because Lean: Prevents waste, Provides value, and, Ensures continuous improvement.

How to utilize analytical information in the Business Service Management Sector

The major difference between a progressing business and a regressing or stagnant one is the ability of the manager to observe, improvise, adapt, and of course, improve. Thousands of businesses have realized this and have subsequently put in as much time as they put into improving their services into analyzing and studying feedback. The increased use of analysis has changed a lot in businesses. Businesses now use analysis to streamline operations which results in improved services and processes which ultimately results in increased profits.

A survey carried out by Bloomberg BusinessWeek Research Services revealed that nearly 97% of the respondent's companies make active use of analytics to reduce costs and increase profits as well as risk management. Without a doubt, the merits of using analytics to grow a business are unequaled and unchallenged. However, problems begin to arise when a business sets about doing it. Realizing progress through the use of analytics is much easier than actually implementing its use.

Understanding Business Intelligence

Business intelligence refers to dealing with technologies and intricate strategies that are used to analyze data. It refers to strategies and applications that use business data to make better business decisions. This analysis helps business owners make better decisions that help grow their businesses in various ramifications. Business intelligence is not a new thing as a popular misconception may claim. Rather, it dates back to 1865. Sir Henry Furnese, a popular banker was said to have made profits by using data gained through environmental analysis to overcome his competitors.

Business intelligence (BI) is very wide. It involves data analytics, big data, and data mining. It also involves a wide array of processes that range from data collection to data sharing and even to reporting. It is these processes that help with decision making. Luckily,

Business intelligence has advanced and so businesses have been equipped with tools that allow them to carry out these processes on their own. Business intelligence deals with data mining, online analytical processing, querying, and reporting. The knowledge gained from these processes is then used to make decisions.

Understanding Service Management:

Service management is often defined as a supply chain management that connects the customer and the company providing goods or services. The aim of service management is to keep inventory levels at a minimum thereby reducing high costs. Service management is totally focused on the customer. Through information technology, service management aims to give the customers what they want thereby strengthening the relationship. Service management does not focus on acquiring a new customer. Rather, it focuses on tightening the hold your business has over that customer. As it is often said, it is far easier to sell to an existing customer than to a new one.

Service management:

- Increases value and cost-efficiency

- Gives managers a clearer view of customer wants and business needs
- Reduces impacts of incidents
- Raises profits
- Reduces money spent on unprofitable products
- Minimizes technician visits

Using Business Intelligence in Service Management:

When Business Intelligence and service management are paired, the result is profit. Together, Business Intelligence and Service Management have bettered the financial aspects of various companies in various aspects. With it, you identify your best selling products as well as information as to why it is your best selling product. With such information, you add the missing ingredient to the rest of your products that do not fare as well. It is basically learning from your own experience.

Before implementing Business Intelligence at all, a company should analyze their current methods of decision making in the service management aspect. What influences the decisions made concerning your services? Then the company needs to think about the information they need that would make their decision-making process rapid and fruitful. You will then need to make a decision on how to present that information. For example, if Joe runs a bar, what would Joe like to know what he thinks would let him know what sorts of liquor to buy, when to buy it, and how to offer it? Joe would then need to decide what way he will arrange that information so that not only he, but all his employees understand. Joe and his employees may feel much more comfortable with a written report as opposed to a softcopy. The information can also be presented in a soft copy, an online tool or some type of chart.

For business intelligence to be used well, it must be explained and demystified in every way. If you run a Google Adsense account, for example, you will notice that apart from showing you what your earnings were on a particular day, Google will show you what your earnings were like a year ago on that same day. That is not enough for Business Intelligence. With Business Intelligence, you must not only provide such data, but you must also give a reason for the rates on each given day. By comparing and contrasting, you will be able to notice the factors that influenced the changes.

In a company, not every employee or worker will be able to fully grasp service management. It is the duty of the business manager to ensure that the decision-making board understands it as they control the workers. For example, if you realize -due to Business Intelligence- that profits went up when you had a particular number of staff on hand as well as some particular products on the ground, it is the job of the manager to pick out the winning factors and make decisions that complement them. The employees are the wheels but you as the manager as the gear; you should direct and they should follow.

However, it should be noted that before any progress can be made through using Analytic Data for Business Intelligence in Service Management, the data must be clean. Clean data, in this case, refers to correct and unadulterated business data. This is a requirement that cannot be bargained.

Using analytic data from business intelligence in service management can be done through:

Obtaining Data:

There are numerous avenues and ways to obtain business-related data. Companies obtain data from the customer and lead information in CRM programs, across social media platforms, sales ledgers, customer reviews, etc. These various sources of data offer information on various aspects of your business. If you are concentrating on service management, draw service-management related data. Business intelligence will find the pattern and trends between that and your profits. Obtaining data from customers can be done in various ways; reviews, surveys, etc. With this, you can obtain the customer sentiment.

Analyzing Data:

When this data has been obtained, it can be analyzed. There are three main types of analytic data; structured data, semi-structured data, and unstructured data. The analyzing of collected data is usually carried out by data warehouses or data marts. Data warehouses are used to align random data into a single central location. Data marts are very similar but carry out their analysis on a smaller scale. For example, rather than analyzing the whole data generated by a company, you can choose to simply deal with data related to service management.

Data marts are cheaper and are easier to implement. This is because they deal with concentrated and specific data. Such data analysis can be carried out by a single person rather than a whole team. As a bonus, it gives a more concentrated analysis. Data warehouses and marts carry receive the data after it has been obtained. The transmission of this data is done through the ETL system. The ETL system stands for Extract, Transform and Load.

Extraction: During extraction, the raw data which has been generated from various sources is extracted. Any structured data is labeled here.

Transformation: All extracted data is made the same. For the data to be analyzed, it must all be in the same format.

Loading: This is the process of transferring the data to the warehouse or mart.

Using Analytic Data for Business Intelligence in Service Management:

The issue of available staff is one that companies deal with quite frequently. With Business Intelligence, you can discover to what extent your business is affected if at all it is. When there is a particular number of staff on ground what are the profits like? How do the customers react? What minimum of number of staff is needed to handle a particular number of customers in order to satisfy them without costing you too much in wages? Where is the balance? Do you fare better with multiple entry-level staff or with a fewer number of experienced ones? At different times with different numbers of staff on hand with different levels of experience, what were the profits like? What were the reviews like? Having the data on hand will give you the ability to answer such questions.

With analyzed data, a business can make decisions concerning inventory stocking. Less money will be wasted as we have a forecast of what performance is going to be like. Teams that deal with service management will be able to predict what it is they need for a certain period. Business Intelligence can present information on how much time is taken to solve a problem. With such information, a manager can study the results in order to reduce the length of time taken in any possible way that optimizes time while giving the same great- or even better if need be- solutions.

Improvements and More Improvements

The aim of Business intelligence is not to give businesses a way of predicting happenings alone; that is secondary. It is mainly to give a clear view of where improvements need to be made. Having such data is invaluable; use it to make improvements and more improvements. Remember that such information is valuable; protect it. A rival company can flatten yours if such private data is leaked. Your Business Intelligence Analytic data is more than just reports. It shows your business's weaknesses and strengths. Be safe.

How do you engage Lean Management in your office?

When an office decides that the way forward is through Lean Analytics, there is a lot to be done. Luckily, there is a lot of knowledge available on lean analytics when it comes to implementing it in the office. When it comes to implementing lean, we can group most of the processes into analyzing and implementing. Yet a wide number of offices do not seem to succeed and its implementation. This is because a lot of time is spent on making use of lean tools rather than thoroughly understanding them. Eager to skip to the best parts, offices ignore the time that has to be put into making sure that the majority of the staff understand and subscribe to the lean ideology.

Another reason why various businesses fail is due to the lean tools are not well directed. The main objective of lean is enabling a company to learn as much as possible as fast as possible which of course, leads to profits. However, sometimes, offices attempt to implement lean without actually explaining to their staff what the aim is and how to achieve that aim, they do not explain the entirety of lean. For lean to work and yield results, it is not simply a matter of implementing the tools into the business, it is a matter of implementing lean into every single office in a business. In other words, it is all to ensure that each office absorbs and processes data about their work-area in large amounts and in superb speeds. It is only when each member of your business is on board with the flow that it can actually be a reality.

With lean management, no department in the office really carries a much larger load. This is because every department that makes up a business has to change the way it runs. A single weak link in the lean chain can negate the effort of others. Each office must know how lean works and what it is to achieve. Lean Analytics is dependent on collective application and alignment. The offices must work together if the implementation of lean will be a reality. Although lean concerns every aspect of an office, it should be concentrated on the offices that directly affect the businesses' speed and ability to deliver. However, the ability of this to happen depends, once again, on collective effort. Delivering services is the last link on a long chain. Each office is a part of that chain. A delay from one point is usually a delay for everyone. With mass and speedy learning, these delays are obliterated.

In each office, the various delays in the rendering of services should be addressed. This includes understanding the problem, seeking out reasons for the delay and finding ways around them. Do customers have to wait for longer periods because they usually request ice in their drinks? Why? How can that be changed? Do customer complaints sit at the table for ages and cause disgruntlement before anything can be done about it? Why? How can that be changed? These are the types of questions that need to be asked and speedily too.

Tips for Implementing Lean Management in Offices:

Carry Your Staff Along:

If your staff are not in agreement or are wary of lean tools due to any reason, it will affect its implementation. Instead of simply giving orders and directives when it comes to lean, explain the reason behind them as well as what you hope to gain. Having them behind you will support you in far more way than you imagined possible. Of course, if you give directives, they will obey you as they work for you but disgruntled staff has a way of getting their own back. Sure, you may insist they say exactly this and that to a customer, you may mandate a smile, but you cannot really cover all bases. It is possible to smile at a customer yet annoy them or make them feel unwelcome. A member of staff can explain a service to a customer in a way that makes them feel stupid. Some customers will speak out and complain. The majority, however, might just walk away and not look back. Theoretical training is important, but it would be wise to not dwell on this. Actualize it and let your staff see exactly how it plays out.

Do not make changes to single departments:

As explained before, the final service rendered is the last link in a long chain. The speed at which that service is rendered depends on every organization. If an organization didn't affect the business, it would not exist. When making changes to departments in a single business or organization follow it up and watch how the change is received. For example, do not just schedule more serving hands for Monday shifts because you have realized business is always packed at those hours. Rather consider if the cooks on hand can actually put out enough food to keep those servers busy who in turn serve as at great speed. You will also need to check if your accounting department can handle the speed at which customers will demand checks or bills as they finish their meals. Of what use are many servers if the food is not prepared on time? Of what use are many servers if the customers are still delayed by waiting for checks. Improper implementation of lean can cause its own problems. Make changes and study the reaction.

Have Steady Departments and Well Defined Output-Standardize:

It is quite impossible to derive structured information if there is no structure. It is quite impossible to implement structured processes if there is no structure. How well structured is your organization? Lack of structure in itself can be a reason for failures in some aspects. Order and structure cannot be done without. It will be hard to learn about each department if duties are not well outlined. Each department should have well outline duties so as to discern where delays often occur.

Once this has been done, it is not important to offer steady output and steady output quality. If your business produces goods, the goods can be periodically tested for quality and assurance. If you provide more services, however, you should take a different approach. Each step to providing the service should be carefully discussed and outlined. The reason sales go up on Tuesdays may be because a particular employee who acts a certain way take is present. That is something the management must discover. Your staff should be given clear instructions on what they are to do and how they are to do it. It may not be enough to say "You are in charge of dealing with customers who come in newly." You may need to set guidelines concerning such things. "Customers must be greeted, offered seats, told this, offered that, etc." Customers should also be informed of what they have access to. This way, no matter the employee, the service quality remains the same. And if you ensure that your customers know what they are entitled to, your staff will watch it. You can also ensure stable service through customer reviews of each staff. If staff are mandated to give their names or wear name tags, coupling that with a review system could provide data.

Balance Quality and Quality:

As a business, before aiming for 50 customers, you should aim for 30 happy customers. This issue is found more in companies providing one-of-a-type services or a new innovation or good. A true business manager realizes that a long-term monopoly is hardly ever a possibility. If you have a new idea for an app, develop it, and then put it out for customers, in less than a month, similar apps will pop up. Customers who only patronized you because of the fact that there were no alternatives will be only too glad to shift camp. It is very hard to gain back a lost customer. Losing customers should not arise; you want them all- no business is complete without them. Direct your lean implementation to every area that affects the quality and watch profits roll in.

Work On Customer Service:

Customer service is one department that has a lot to do. This is because they deal directly with your clients and customers. Fran who didn't wrap the package well will not have to deal with angry Karen. Rather customer service agent Janet who knows nothing about it will receive the full wrath of Karen's displeasure. This is another advantage of letting everyone know who handles what and at least a brief summary of how it should be handled. With such knowledge, it is easier to placate customers. Your customer service should be efficient and trained. A customer-service staff should be trained in order to enable them to deal with the customers well. Some customers are nightmares however, except they go against our business's values, we still want their patronage. And so, a lot must be borne.

A trained customer service agent will also exude warmth and confidence that will comfort current customers and attract new ones. The customer service department may affect your profits more than the department that actually produces the service or goods. It is not something new for a customer to shun a service simply because of the nonchalant, lazy, and sometimes even mean and uncaring service they will receive from the customer service. Successful businesses have strong customer service departments.

Think Outside the Box:

Lastly, think outside the box. Lean analytics focuses on learning large information at a fast rate. With this information, decisions are made. Following conventional methods is not the only way there is. Brainstorm ideas. Have your staff present a solution alongside any problem they encounter. Deliberate on decisions slowly and make them only after careful research but once that is one, implement them as fast as possible.

The Lean Manufacturing tools and how to effectively use them

Lean manufacturing tools are tools or rather methods that are used to help companies learn large amounts of information in little time. This is done in order to exterminate wasted time and resources thus making the manufacturing workflow a 'lean' one. Let's look at some of the important lean tools, their aims, and how to make the most out of them.

The Five Whys:

The five why's is a method to determine the root cause of a problem by asking the question why 5 times. Often times, we may not even need to reach the five-mark before the cause is revealed. This lean tool, developed by Sakichichi Toyoda, is usually carried out by teams to jointly discover roots of problems. Often at times, we tackle the wrong area and get frustrated when profits are not as they should be. We may tackle the area of marketing and publicity when the actual problem is quality. The five whys will discover root problems and connected problems.

Making the Most of the Five Whys:

In order to use this tool effectively, ensure that:

You have knowledgeable persons about the subject matter on the discussion team. If the problem concerns a certain department every member, if possible, should be present in order to drop their two-bit. The members of the team should understand the problem and what is to be done. They must be knowledgeable.

Make use of this tool in a hardcopy form. Rather than computers, make use of pen and paper or a board and marker.

Ensure that the questions are answered step by step; do not jump the gun and skip a cause.

Make it an interactive meeting. If each person is able to contribute freely but orderly, you will learn new things. The real reason you gain the most negative reviews on Wednesday may not be because of the chefs in the back but because of the servers. The real reason production is at the lowest point on Fridays may not be because the machines have been running all week but because the workers on Fridays are relatively inexperienced.

Each answer to a why should be generally agreed on my majority. The best way this can be done is to ensure that each why is answered through logic and should be backed up by facts.

Answer questions from the customers' viewpoint and not just yours.

One-Piece Flow [Continuous Flow]:

One-piece flow is also known as a continuous flow. It is a lean tool that focuses on the manufacturing aspect of a business. This tool eliminates large-amount processing. It directs processing to be grouped into smaller batches. That is groups are formed and they manufacture smaller amounts per group. The aim of this is to enable a detailed examination of output. This information is quickly learned and is passed onto the next batch that can then make improve their methods in relation to what the preceding batch learned. One Piece or Continuous-flow aims to work, observe, learn, adapt and do it all over again. Think of it this way; a baker who has an order for a thousand loaves of bread decides to bake the first batch of just fifty. After the first batch is done, he has some unbiased people taste the bread and give him feedback. He also takes stock of the ingredients he used and if any was wasted in the batch of fifty. From the feedback on the taste, he can adjust his recipe and from his own feedback on measurements, he can adjust his scales. Next, he makes another batch and redoes the process.

Making The Most of One Piece or Continuous Flow of order:

To make the most out of this tool, ensure that:

Examination tools for the work of each batch are put in place.

There are tools put in place to make necessary adjustments according to feedback.

The manufactures focus only on manufacturing and receiving orders.

You set up a department for analyzing reports on each batch produced.

You have another department that will focus on implementing the changes as efficiently [monetary and time] as possible.

You generally reduce the work in each step as much as possible

The teams involved have a joint meeting to assess progress. Nothing encourages workers as much as seeing that they are actually making progress.

Cellular Manufacturing:

Cellular Manufacturing has to do with each business having its units arrange their departments based on what they produce. In cellular manufacturing, similar departments are grouped together. This is done mainly to eliminate delays in transmission. In the manufacturing sector, the departments are placed closely together so that they have access to each other. Departments should be arranged based on the flow of services. Take a drink manufacturing company. The workstation where bottles are cleaned and deemed okay for use should be placed next to the department that fills them and then to where they are corked then lastly to where they are labelled. Depending on whatever workflow your business has, arrange your departments. That way, there are no interruptions.

Making the Most of Cellular Manufacturing:

To use this tool efficiently, ensure that:

The workflow of a company is thoroughly understood by you. It is not enough to know it in theory. Theoretically, the label on drink bottles may be due to be placed after the bottle is washed but realistically, the labels take much longer to be made and so the workers just end up using the labels last. Adopt that as the original workflow and rearrange the workstation in accordance with that.

Work on the methods of transportation between workstations. How does the product get to each workstation? Is it efficient? Why, why, why, why and why is what you need to ask yourself.

Call meetings privately with each manufacturing workstation. Each unit is sure to face some difficulties related to the networking that should take place between the various workstations. These pieces of information should be analyzed.

Call general meetings with all workstations. Brainstorm together. Remember that you should not make changes to single departments without follow up on how it affects other departments.

Continuous Improvement:

The name gives this lean tool away. Continuous improvement dwells on the steps taken to directly improve the efficiency of your services. Continuous Improvement is related to every part of a business. Continuous improvement works towards improving the efficiency of time, the efficiency of workstations, and the efficiency of money. It also deals with the proper management of resources. The general aim is to ensure that progress is being made in every ramification. If progress is indeed being made, profits are bound to follow. Continuous improvement must be implemented religiously.

Making the Most of Continuous Improvement:

In order to make the most out of this tool, ensure that:

The problem is detected. Once you find out what needs to improve you are making a problem. A problem discovered is one half-solved.

A full proof plan is created. Now, a plan for improvement can hardly be full-proof at the first try as you will always discover ways to better it. However, at the time the plan is made and the decision to implement it is made, there should be no visible problems with the plot.

Once the plan is put into motion, it is time to study its outcome. Here, data can be collected on its performance.

The performance is studied in order to make improvements where necessary.

When a better plan is created, implement it fully and as swiftly as possible.

Total Productive Maintenance:

Total productive maintenance deals with manufacturing tools. Some say that a worker is only as good as his tools. In this case, it is very right. If the machines are faulty, your speed will be affected. Total productive management [sometimes referred to a TPM] deals with ensuring that the machines are properly maintained to avoid breakdowns. TPM also strives to safeguard workers against incidents that can happen as a result of faulty machines. It deals with preventive, corrective and constructive maintenance. TPM is used alongside the OEE metric. OEE stands for Overall Equipment Effectiveness. This ensures that a machine is actually productive when its total working time is calculated.

Making the Most of Total Productive Maintenance TPM

In order to enjoy the maximum output from this tool, ensure that:

You buy only quality machines that are needed and are of good quality. With production, you cannot afford to buy a machine meant for one purpose and use it permanently for another

Machines are scheduled for check-ups and are repaired as soon as they develop a fault. Do you know that it saves money by attending to a problem as soon as it arrives and before it aggravates? A stitch in time saves nine.

Before each use machines are checked.

A meeting is held where workers can explain the difficulties they experience with various machines. Deem if that can be changed. If it can, change it.

How you can use Lean Analytics in your Company

Lean analytics deals with building, analyzing, learning, and improving. However, for lean analytics to work for your company, it has to be done right. Companies give up on Lean Analytics as a result of seeing no results due to improper implementation.

Before you implement lean analytic, decide what type of business you run. What are the things that you know in and about your business, really? The answer to that question should be "A Lot" as you are going to need a large amount of knowledge. Lean analytics works on knowledge of your business which you have and does not teach you about your business. You must then decide how progressed your business is? Businesses go through 5 stages:

Empathy:

Realizing a need and deciding to solve it. When this is done, a company creates a product with the intent of solving the problem.

Stickiness:

At this point, you throw your product into the market to test the reaction. This is the stage where you notice whether if now people actually buy it.

Virality:

This is where you bother about acquiring customers. Here acquiring customers indicates that they are coming back for more.

Revenue:

In this stage, profits are involved. The main of a business is to make money and so you put things in place to ensure that your product is making money.

Scale:

The last stage is all about expansion. As profits come in, your thoughts are on how to sell more and acquire even more profit.

At each stage of this process, data is collected. However, using tools to analyze this data is what lean analytics is about. From the onset, of course, you should ensure you have clean data that has not been influenced in anyways it should not be. The collected data are your business metrics. Business metrics are measurable data that businesses use to analyze the failure or success of various decisions taken. Metrics are either quantitative or qualitative. Qualitative metrics focus on value and quantitative on the amount.

A good metric must be:

Measurable in order to compare: Metrics are valued for measurement and comparison sake. Your metric data's use cannot be fully actualized if it cannot be compared. The information lies in the comparisons made. From the comparison, you can ask and answer questions about just how well your company is faring.

It should be expressed in ratio: We express metrics in ratio to other metrics. It is much better to state profit levels and also state them in ratio to profits at this same time a year or month ago than to just state profit levels.

Easy to understand: Businessmen who make use of metrics are people who specialize in making money and not reading data. If a businessman with little to no prior knowledge of analytics is to use metrics, it must be easy to understand.

Understanding KPIs:

KPI means Key Performance Metric. KPI are metrics that carry out assessment and analysis of a Company's manufacturing efficiency. They are metrics that help you measure where you are and where you want to be. Some types of KPIs are speed and quantity. Speed metrics bother about time efficiency while quantity bothers about the amount. Reject ratio is another KPI that deals with waste.

There are seven types of waste:

Overproduction: This is more common and refers to the production of more than what is needed. Overproduction wastes production resources.

Rejected production: If a product cannot be used because of an error, it is wasted. Hence, waste occurs.

Inappropriate processing methods: Remember how we spoke about using the right machine for the right job? Well, when you use a wrong machine that is more expensive to run for a particular job for something that could be less, it is a waste.

Excessive movement: When a worker has to move too much, it wastes time and reduces the efficiency

Waiting: If excess time is spent between the end of one production and the beginning of the next, waste has occurred.

Excess Transportation: Transportation is the means of getting the product to the customer. However, if a product is moved around more than it should be, if a product takes more time to be delivered than it would on a standard route, waste has occurred. It is an excessive movement for both vehicles and humans.

Unnecessary inventory: Having unwanted goods on the ground is the last form of waste.

Metrics reveal the truth behind every aspect of a business, it is invaluable. However, data should work for you and not the other way around. You should not make a decision based on data but based on the analysis of data. It is not really difficult. Data should guide your decision making and not dictate it.

A common reason businesses fail is trying to do everything at once. As suggested by Alistair Croll and Benjamin Yoskovitz, find one important metric and focus on it. When you focus on one metric, it is easy to control what goes on. It allows you to learn, analyze, and solve in an orderly manner.

Understanding the Lean Analytics Cycle:

As we now understand, lean analytics deals with building, analyzing, learning, and improving. It is analyzing, learning, and improving to become a continuous cycle. The last stage of the cycle, improving, is where depends on the implementation.

Improving From Learning:

When you learn, you find out what needs to be improved. This is why you need to understand your business as we spoke about before. Lean analytics acts as a builder. However, it needs a foundation which is your knowledge about your business. Once this is done, you can focus on metrics. You can combine metrics from your business with metrics from other related businesses. When this is done, you focus on a singular metric and decide where improvements need to be made.

Be Creative with Possible Solutions:

Using the various lean tools, you can get to the root cause of your problem and come up with solutions. Now it is time to think out of the box. Although you are to be creative, these solutions are not to come off the top of your head. Your solutions should be created after carrying out research. Now that you have a problem, find out why. If you know your business that well, you should know if it a common one or if it is a peculiar one. Carry our research on both larger and smaller-scale companies who perform the same functions as you. If you have suitable data, it will be easier to discover key factors causing the issues. Coming up with solutions is usually a team duty. Managers and business owners have found it benefitting to have their employees brainstorm along with them. However, ultimately you hold the veto power and your employees can only suggest.

Implement Your Solutions on A Small Scale:

Remember that your solution is still theoretical. It is not proven. A genuine as your data and analyzes may be, it may simply not just work. This is not the fault of the tools but rather the fault of the chosen solution. The great thing about this stage is, either way, you win. If your solution turns out suitable, you have a problem solved. If it does not, you have not only learned, you have also acquired more data. Have a clear view of what your solution is to achieve. After that is done, you can move on to implementing it on a smaller scale as it is still a test.

Study the Outcomes:

This is when you need to sit back and watch. You are to measure the outcome of the experiment. If your chosen, solution solves the problem, you have succeeded. You can now move on to the next metric and solve the next problem. If your solution did not perform as expected, it is back to the drawing board.

Depending on the outcome, you may need to revise and edit your solution or throw it away.

When attempting to implement lean analytics into your company, pay attention to the PCDA Cycle.

PDCA Problem Solving Cycle:

PCDA is a lean analytics tool which stands for Plan, Do, Check, and Act. It is identical to what we discussed above. PCDA comes into play when a problem needs to be solved. With PCDA, problems are solved orderly.

Plan: The planning stage is the stage of identifying the problem and creating a solution. Your solution should be detailed.

Do: Here your plan is carried out on a small scale.

Check: The outcome of the test is analyzed.

Act: If it failed, you start the cycle again. If it doesn't you implement on a wide scale. You must act fast.

Points to Remember when implementing lean analytics:

Ensure you know more than enough about your business

Ensure that you understand the lean analytics tool you'll be using

Ensure that your staff is carried along as much as is possible

Work in the Public Sector: How important is Lean Training?

One of the biggest questions to really answer is how to merge Lean into the training requirements of the public sector seeing they run on a different template than what Lean might offer. We could rather ask how a public sector run organization can merge the timeless principles present in Lean into their organization. Whether it is private or public sector; the customer/target audience/consumer is the prima donna, the primary focus of it all. That means there should be no room for too many mistakes with reaching your targeted customers.

The public sector unlike private is service-driven; its aim is to serve the people more than getting remunerations. That's why it could seem out of place to think that lean could be applied to the public sector just like it can be applied to the private sector. The public sector is run on taxes unlike the private that is revenue-driven. The public sector is designed to serve like government parastatal, schools and other public paraphernalia. Even the way employment occurs in the public sector is quite different from how it happens in the private sector. In the public sector, employment is designed so that government work can go on, and public offices could run. The police officers, teachers, fire-fighters, etc. are all types of public sector employment. The way staff gets paid is through taxes and internal or externally generated revenue—but majorly taxes.

In the UK, for instance, the size of the public sector is 17% of the entire workable population—that is, 17% of everyone who is appropriate and eligible for work or can be classified in the workforce category of the society all work in the public sector. In February 2016, the central government received £53.1bn in income and spent £57.1bn, and two-thirds of all that was spent in departments under the central government like; health, education, and defense.

Whether private or public sector, every customer wants to be satisfied with the services you render and we realized we can apply the lean principle to running your public sector office. The issue of service becomes a bigger problem because the government is involved and the people want to get a benefit of their taxes.

Norman Flynn the British writer said in his book public sector management, Alden press UK in 2007, that there is "a clear distinction must be made in the provision of services by the public and private sectors. The public sector does not sell goods or services to people at a profit; nor are these same goods and services withheld from people who cannot afford to pay for them. The raison-d-etre of the public sector is based on the premise that it is not money-oriented machinery; its role is to provide protection, to help those in need, and educate"

His point is as clear as crystal, public sector funds are used to render more services. The public sector should be focused on rendering services. The public sector should create a business climate that ensures that the private sector is run properly.

The lean process was born in the manufacturing sector with the likes of Ford Motor Company and Toyota leaning the trail. It was designed in order to synchronize work processes, limit waste, and Increase Company's ROI. In short, it was designed to ensure that organizations were doing more with less. The public sector is beginning to have its fair share of the cake as most public sector organizations now practice the lean methodology or at least have processes that resemble it.

In 1988, the Baldridge Award stretched its bounds to the involved public sector. They also made moves that suggested the inclusion of lean methods to public sector processes; like the establishment of the Federal Quality Institute in 1988 that was designed to facilitate the improvement of the process throughout government and to ensure that there is an upgrade in the total quality management of these government processes. Also, the reinventing of the government as heralded by the Clinton/gore combo; the ultimate objective was to make sure the government has more output with less input. It is the overall aim of lean to ensure that public organizations do more with less.

Lean allows organizations to break down their processes into components and monitors each component analytically. This would lean to the management of organization resource because the organization can see clearly areas that they can improve on, improvise or cut out. If work process is broken into fragments, it becomes easier to monitor than holistically. A holistic view is good when drawing out the plan and vision for the organization, but when execution is concerned, it is the tiny fragments that matter. Those little chips you cannot see make a device function and that's what lean brings to the fore; the importance of these little fragments and how they influence the flow of resources in an organization; whether public or private. Lean methods view efficiency from the end user's perspective; that, what the end-user defines as value. Whatever process eradicates waste and delivers the value the end-user desires is the best process. From the spotting of the need, to the choice of staff to handle the task, to the resources available for the execution to the process of approval, the time take, the effect of the project on the community all can come under the lens of lean and the best approach devised to conserve resources and have the best output.

Define measure, analyze, improve, and control the outcome of the project—these are simple steps that can be applied to ensure an organization functions at its optimum when delivering a product. Defining and measuring entails a careful perusal of the hitches that hinder the process of delivering the service and the extent of damage. Analyzes involve the careful examination of why things went wrong. Improve involves the steps the organization would take to ensure that these problems do not resurface; it's an evolution of the system and it's processes. Control finally involves setting up frameworks that allow the improved idea work.

Should public offices invest in lean training?

For every organism to thrive in its environment, the organism must learn and evolve. Any organization that refuses to learn, unlearn and relearn would soon be obsolete. Human wants are becoming more complex; our needs are getting more insatiable. We just are not satisfied with what is handed over to us. What about speed? The rate at which things react in the 21st century is alarming; it is needed for speed in real life now. Everything is moving on a fast lane. The need to constantly evolve to face these new needs is increasing and the best way to grow is to get acquiesced with this new world. You need to get trained; the whole organization needs an overhaul, if not you would be practicing processes that don't have the capacity to solve client needs.

If you found a way to improve your system and workflow process, why won't you latch on to it? The lean methodology affords you the opportunity to use timeless methods to solve company problems, conserve energy, conserve resources and save time.

With this training you can improve customer satisfaction: the customer is the reason why people do business. The citizen is the reason for the creation of the public office; the citizen is the focus of the public office. Every public office should pride in the fact that projects are carried out to meet the needs of the citizen even more, the needs of the community. That's how every public office is evaluated.

Through this training, you would experience improved staff morale, and staff engagement; If your staff should understand you don't just care about what they give to you, but what you can also give to them, they would be encouraged to see the organization not just as an organization, but as their own. You would inevitably impact staff engagement through training because they would be put in an environment that can allow them to express themselves and discover things about themselves that they might not have known. The lean methodologies can be applied to personal lives; you would have given them an opportunity to be better persons through the training process.

Increased revenue is a sure bet: a framework that can streamline your workflow process to tiny bits that can be monitored, which would invariably impact the quality of products that are delivered because the system is obvious and streamlined. It would also save you from wastes; (I think this is one point that has been reiterated in this book a lot; it ought to sink) we can't explain this enough. It is imperative that for any organization to thrive, the organization should be able to curb wastes and overhead costs. Lean methodology endows you with the skill through a very effective framework. This framework would affect revenue. Let's streamline this to public office if the process can guarantee a reduction in lead time, increased productivity, lower costs, and improved staff engagement, the economy would be impacted; that means it would be easier to do business because the climate would be healthier. If public offices are effective, then the economy would be affected and there would be an increase in revenue.

Lean has easy to understand tools that any organization can master in no time. Every public office should apply these principles because of how effective it is.

Common mistake to avoid while using Lean in your Office

Lean in a company's start-ups, as observed, can be of great benefit to companies, especially start-ups. The series of processes involved in Lean implementation has been known not just only to promote corporate effectiveness but also build people's development and communication. Little wonder several companies are adopting the Lean plan today, including start-ups; Start-ups being businesses at their fresh start. The Lean mechanism has been so simplified and made applicable to virtually all kinds of businesses. And with its high success rating, it is almost irresistible to Start-ups.

Start-ups are no more skeptical about plunging into the business sphere; it is like their easy guarantee to business success. It almost seems like the Lean plan is the ideal beginner's model plan. But then, we must be made to realize that there is no ideal or perfect business plan. The plan could be all the way perfect, up until its implementation and actualization. Even in the Lean business plan, things could go wrong in its implementation irrespective of how good and ideal it looks on paper? Because the ultimate question to ask after all is, "who is responsible for the application and implementation of these strategies??" Multi-purpose robots and advanced technology? Certainly not! The Lean strategy is more of a traditional strategy than technological or supernormal, believe it or not! Humans run the operations in Lean strategies, and that alone entails the inevitability of loopholes. These loopholes are prevalent from the plan drafting stage to the supposed "victory" stage. They are common and "not so dire" mistakes that can be avoided. We are going to be studying and unmasking these loopholes under the radar of start-up companies. They are new, they are fresh, seemingly amateurs in the business. They are much more prone to these mistakes than already existing businesses. This is a survival guide, a helpful tool to help start-ups make the right decisions and tow the right paths towards achieving Lean success, as I would call it. Now, what are these things that could go wrong? What should start-ups watch out for?

Not Having a Big Compelling Vision:

It is only logical to think that every and any business before starting up should have a big vision. A Compelling big vision is what steers your cause as an entrepreneur or a start-up. The company's vision is like a compass, keeping everyone faced in the right direction. Everyone knows what the company expects to see in the future to come and work collaboratively to see it happen. Your company's vision and type should also affect your Lean strategy. When you know what you want to see and have the brainpower to make it happen, your strategies will be slightly different from that of a company with a different vision, though it is the same lean business model. The ideas you come up with will be all geared towards achieving your vision with the Lean model. Many start-ups today are using the Lean framework as an excuse not to have a vision. After all, it is such an easy to initiate a start-up to days; Tons of people are doing it!

Now let us set something straight; Lean strategy is more like a means to an end, not the end in itself. Start-ups should of utmost importance learn to see lean strategies as processes that help them move towards achieving their vision or goal. The strategy is not the product; it is just a tool you build to know what product to build. Your vision allows you to be open to new possibilities, even within the Lean framework. Furthermore, starting a company without a vision leaves you bare and susceptible to outside influences, from customers, investors, competition, press, and everything else. It leaves you without a purpose, over time, you will find yourself wandering, trying out "whatever works." The role of lean Analytics is to expand your vision; for expansion to occur, a vision must exist. Lean does not help you create a vision for your business.

Lack of Readiness and unpreparedness (Not asking the right questions):

Starting up a business is a big decision and takes a lot. Before ever initiating a start-up, there are a few questions entrepreneurs need to ask themselves;

The first question should be, "Can I do this thing I am hoping to do, well?" Here you need to assess your ability in comparison with what you are seemingly up against. Little reminder; while you are identifying a problem and cracking up solutions for them, some other persons are identifying the same problems too or already have a system in place to meet the need already; the odds cannot be overlooked. Now the question you need to ask yourself is this; "What do you have to bring to the table that your competition does not have already or has not presented at the table? It cannot possibly be just mere conventional dreams and visions in the paper! Do you have a network of friends or contacts that can improve your odds? From your design skills to coding to branding, everything needs to fresh and different. Let your innovative mindset come to play!

The next question is, "Do I like what I am doing?" Now it is of the essence to know that start-ups are very tasking. They burn up so much time. The time that's supposed to be spent with friends, partner, children (as the case may be), even your hobbies. Something has to go in for something.

All these will inadvertently get to be sacrificed in the formative stage of every business (starting up). This is why this question is very crucial. It takes something you love so much to seemingly take the place of other things you may like even more. If your heart's not in it, you will not give your all for it; no 100% commitment and dedication. Is it a problem worth solving and worth the trouble? If you were paid nothing at all to do this same thing, will you jump at the offer? These are some of the questions you need to ask yourself before starting up with anything. If the answer to these questions is NO, then keep looking! You have not found the problem for you to solve yet!

Then the final question; "will I make money doing it?". You need to give the market what they need, not what you think they need. Give them the value they can pay anything for in the most cost-efficient way possible. The idea behind making a product was to meet a need, not rank top list in the hall of fame for "GENIUS IDEAS NO ONE NEEDS."

These are questions an entrepreneur should ask himself before starting up a venture. Lean Analytics method or business models have no part to play in this. They do not answer the questions for you. Most start-ups were built without the entrepreneur sitting down to think these questions through. Then they try to employ lean-to magically make up for or salvage their bad decisions or business unpreparedness and ill planning. Lean strategies barely work out for these because there were no afterthoughts to the selection of a product to come up with and no passion or commitment to keep the venture going when it does not work out the first few times. Lean strategies are not full-proof on their own; the hands implementing them tend to be responsible for how fast or how slow the plans get to yield results. For start-ups like this, the ride would be a rather long one!

Hiring inexperienced project managers/ Title and Job Monopoly:

The lean strategy is a very critical framework, thereby requiring a high level of experience and leadership skills. It is indisputable that it takes very ardent leadership skills, and not just that, a certain level of experience to get people driving towards an achievable or seemingly unachievable goal. No matter how talented or skilled a team is, they can barely achieve much under an inexperienced or overburdened project manager. Someone has to set the pace, get the ball rolling! Now, to the entrepreneur, starting up a business does not mean you have to run it by yourself as well. Lean business models cannot be managed by just anyone with no knowledge or experience on how to implement the Lean plan. A project manager has to be hired in the event of the entrepreneur not having the prerequisite knowledge needed to achieve the Lean program. A team should also be set in place. Do not make a mistake as an entrepreneur to own the task of heading the Lean business team knowing you do not have what it takes; the experience and all. Let someone fill the shoes; your company is still yours. The plan is to get it moving fine, not so? Another mistake a start-up could make; work monopoly. Do not forget that the Lean strategy is a team strategy. One man cannot do all the work. An entrepreneur should proceed to hire a team.

Also, for start-ups, trying to utilize and conserve resources and finances, what seems ideal would be to hire an inexpensive project manager. Here is another problem. This temptation is almost legitimate. But unless you consider of more importance stacking up finances to achieving significant outputs, this temptation should not be given in to. Experienced Lean project managers know how to motivate, encourage, and inspire a team. Inexperienced project managers may have the knowledge, know how to work the tools, know the rules, the strategies, and be capable of drafting the best plans. But beyond that, a project manager should be able to employ empathy, compassion, and know the basic rudiments of the human relationship to promote effectiveness. Ever heard of the proverbial "blind leading the blind to safety"? A newbie should never take the spot of the project manager, especially with no leadership skills whatsoever. Getting people to work is not done by swinging some magic wand. To achieve maximum success in a lean plan, everyone must work just as hard. Now being a start-up, it is obvious your pay is not going to be as good as the others in the business; no profit is coming in yet, so cutting costs seems like an ultimate strategy, maybe even employing fewer hands, meaning more work for one individual. Now, what is going to make these ones stay even under such "not so enticing" conditions? Your team head, the project manager. The project manager has the responsibility of drowning himself in the company's vision and target and devising the best means possible to get the hearts of the team members sold to the company's cause as well. Only then can significant progress be seen; when everyone is working because they have bought into the vision and love what they are doing, not just because they have to leave the house every morning and need to earn a little to feed their bellies.

Focusing more on the tools than the people development:

The lean strategy is not a self-dependent or entirely digital strategy. What do I mean by this? The Lean approach, like many other strategies, requires humans for implementation. Other than that, it is just a beautiful plan, with prospects lying waste on a whiteboard or piece of paper. It does not make itself happen.

Another common mistake start-ups are prone to make shifting all the focus from everything else to just the tools outlined in this strategy. "Everything else" here encapsulates people's development and building. The Lean is a leadership philosophy rather than a methodology, and its success can be primarily attributed to the leadership style rather than the tools involved in the process.

What can your people offer at this point? How far can they go to make this happen? Do they have the right knowledge and skills to make this happen? However, perfect your strategy may be, however, detailed; the people either create it or kill it. Every vision flourishes in the right hand. So to start-ups, what answer do you have to this question; "what are your plans towards people development? Developing the team, you operate with?" Most start-ups have no answer to this question. Some have never even thought about it or considered it vital.

"Grow the people and watch the vision grow" striving to grow the vision without increasing the people is like watering the leaves with no regard to the root. The root is the life source and support of the tree or plant; it keeps it standing.

Also, there is an aspect of customer development. Lean is mostly dependent on customer feedback. Favorable customer feedback should be a priority to start-ups. Feedbacks should be gotten in any way possible, even directly from customers or phone calls. How to know a start-up that is doomed for failure? They neglect the needs of their customers. This is not even logical, but it happens. I mean, you are in the business because you wanted to meet my needs as a customer; you should be concerned that my needs are not being met; unless you got into the market for the wrong reasons. Value creation should be foremost on the minds of Start-ups, creating value the customers cannot resist, letting them give you an opinion on how your product makes them feel, that is, good customer retention strategy! Let them know you are in the business to keep them satisfied and lighten their burden. Start-ups should, as much as possible, commit their time to build their customer base. It is an essential tool in Lean methods.

Adopting another company's Lean plan and expecting it to work:

 This is another danger inherent in having inexperienced project managers and not developing your team as they ought to be developed. The Lean strategy has various levels of implementation. As a matter of fact, it specifies different stages and levels of company growth and pinpoints that of a necessity, a company should know what stage she currently is at every point in time and as the ladder progresses. Inexperienced project managers in a bid to shield their incompetence would quickly settle for the "Copy and paste" mechanism. This is how they think; "It worked for Company A; there is no cogent reason why it should not work for us too!" Hey mister! There are cogent reasons. It is never advisable to adopt another company's Lean plan for yours. Your Lean business model should consider the customers and their buying process too. You should ask yourself questions like; How customers buy your product, why they purchase from you, at which stage of your business they are in, and what the budget of your customer is before building your Lean business model. Your business model should work best for your customers. Start-ups should understand this and not be in a hurry to fly the kites above the cloud level.

Building your own Lean business model also helps you determine your OMTM (One Metric that Matters) you should know which metric to be used at which stage of business. Focus is critical; if you distribute your attention to different parameters, then you will be directed ahead of learning. Every step requires one metric that needs to be worked on. Select that particular metric to work with and fix your target after conducting the necessary research.

For example, a company has it's metric as Churn (customer's complaints). Then consequently, they set a target to ensure that the churn rate does not go beyond 3%. Now, if the churn rate is less than or equal to 3%, for them, success is achieved because they have hit their goal. Owning your own business plan helps you know the metric and target for the moment and helps everyone further channel all their focus into achieving that. Only then can the company be said to be experiencing Lean progress?

Also, I know that every company is different; in terms of business type. The type of business modifies the strategies employed to implement the Lean approach. For instance, some companies have online-based markets. For this kind of company, their plans are going to be invariably different from those of companies whose demands are not online-based. Companies also have different market targets. The customers I am trying to reach out to might be totally different from yours. For instance, one company may be focused on reaching out to the elderly populace while another might have their focus on younger people. Almost everything about their strategies will not be the same.

Presumably, in a stage such as the Virality stage, where we are focusing on customer retention, all strategies employed by the company looking at the elderly market would be more traditional and "just right" but for the company with the target of reaching out to the younger populace, fresh, extreme and "out of the box" ideas are an added plus. Also, branding for a company with its target as the female populace will be entirely different from that of companies with their objective being the male populace. All these are reasons why a company should never copy another company's business plan. Your plan should be suited to work just for you!

Now, let us be clear on something; lean plans are different from strategies. The program is there, as we have studied. The procedures are just simple ways and things to do to see this plan implemented. Now as much as it is very wrong to adopt another company's Lean policy, and strategies for company types that are different from yours and which have different visions and targets are not your best bet at achieving success, it is also viable for companies to take a peek into their competitor's strategies and maybe adopt them. Their competitors are the companies that are of the same type are theirs with very similar targets. Knowing that these ones have been in the industry probably longer than you have, some of their strategies might be beneficial to you, especially if these strategies were responsible for plummeting them to where they are at the moment; look for the successful competitors to learn from. Once you have discovered these strategies, you could either just apply them or modify them and make them even better to get better results than they did. Start-ups should learn from this too. Be confident, but not overconfident; it could be harmful to your business.

*Skipping the steps: Now, we are aware that there are beautiful inherent steps to follow in the Lean procedure. These steps follow a sequence and are classified, thus; Empathy, Stickiness, Virality, Revenue, and Scale.

In the first stage; Empathy, the goal is to find a problem for which people are begging a solution.

In the second stage, Stickiness demands that you create an MVP product to solve that problem you found. What is an MVP (Minimum viable product)? It is a product just enough to satisfy early customers and provide feedback for future product development. It is like the "test product." The goal at this stage is customer feedback and retention.

In the next stage, Virality aims at getting customers in the most cost-efficient way and keeping them. Like the name implies, making the product go viral! Possibly the improved version, if there was the need for that from the feedbacks gotten.

In the fourth stage now, you can begin to calculate your revenue and do Economics work. Start keeping tabs on cash inflow. Monetize your enterprise.

In the fifth stage, plans are now made to grow the business, expand your horizon. This is beyond the lean method.

For start-ups, these stages could be broadened into stages such as problem validation, solution creation, and validation and so on.

Now, why did I take my time to highlight these stages of lean Analytics? Watch the progress, examine the sequence; this is where most start-ups get it wrong again. Some start-ups begin to place emphasis on the Economics and Revenue, which, as we have seen, goes all the way up to the fourth stage of Lean analytics. They want to start calculating their revenue already, hoping to make up for start-up capital. Hey!! Here is a wake-up call!, Pearls don't grow on trees! In Lean Analytics, every stage is mandatory, and following these stages, sequentially, is the only sure bet to achieving success. You have to follow the manual to operate the machine.

Some start-ups also get it wrong at the first and second stages; it is clearly stated; "find a problem, find a solution (a product)." So many start-ups want to be the Jack of all trades. "There are so many problems, and I have solutions to all. Let us just dive into the several and see which one pays best!" Really; Building a single product and getting it all the way up to stage five is already a hardball to roll. Now rolling several at once, that is tantamount to knocking yourself down from so many angles. There is no disputing it, you are going to fall, and very hard at that! Focus on the topmost need, build a product, and focus on building that first. Let your eggs all be in one basket at this time; it keeps you focused on ensuring that one basket is out of harm's way. Channel your full energy there and see maximum results.

Also, know that your MVP is like a test sample; it will be liable to many criticisms from customers. Fewer objections may arise after the first few adjustments and advancements, but almost at every point, there will be criticisms. People would surely have something to say; it could just be the branding/packaging. Whatever happens, never take criticisms personal. It is a necessary part of the steps most start-ups do not understand. There are constructive ones; see them as an opportunity and drive to get better, not as an attack on your person and establishment. Work on as much of them as you can at the moment. You have to give the customers what they want to make them part of their finances. I cannot, as a customer, pay for what does not appeal to me.

*Not Inclusive Enough: Lean project management is a management framework that is inherently collaborative. It is inclusive by nature. Different departments need to be in communication to work and project the Lean analytics plan effectively. In addition, team members need to be able to talk honestly and openly, share ideas without undue criticisms. Despite the fact that a project manager would be in place, the Lean strategy is never a one-man show. However, good a project manager may be, and whatever level of experience he might have had over the years, there is always room for new and fresh ideas on how to propel the lean analytics business model. That is why there is a team; the project manager cannot think of every possible option at the same time. He is just one person and as such, is limited. Everyone is saddled with the responsibility of churning out fresh and productive ideas for review by the rest of the team. What happens during the review? The achievability of the idea is weighed under certain parameters having the company's vision in mind. Is it going to jeopardize the company's vision and target? What are the pros? What are the cons? Do we have the resources and manpower as a company to make this work? It is okay to have your idea not taken, especially when you are given reasons why it cannot be feasible. What's more? You analyzed its feasibility too, alongside everyone else. They made you see those risks and pit holes you did not see while reviewing the plan as one person. This is why teamwork cannot be overemphasized. Now, where do start-ups get this wrong? They get it wrong in leaving the sole innovative and decisive task for one man.

In a lean Analytics team where one man stands to be unopposed, progress may be stagnant. People should never be made to feel their inputs do not matter. It is like shutting down the brain circuits of everyone in the team, leaving them as "yes buddies," just agreeing with whatever the Genius comes up with. A lean team should be all-inclusive; everyone must be on board whatever actions that are to be taken, and every input or dispute must be put into significant consideration. Without honest communication and transparency, lean projects could never thrive. All plans towards hitting the target could be diversified and shared amongst little groups of twos and threes.

Conclusively on this, Lean projects thrive when project managers encourage everyone to give their input, regardless of their rank, title, or experience. Every team member should be valued; everyone must be "all hands and brains in"! No one should be left to rot on the side-lines; everyone has a measure of value to offer. Lean team members consequently grow in confidence in their own abilities. They now have the "we can do anything" mindset. This helps the company's growth in tons.

Spotting a Good metric with the right characteristics and Adaptability:

A Good metric can be described as one that suits whatever stage a company finds itself in at any point in time. Metrics vary, just as the stages in company advancements vary. A good metric is just as important as the Lean model plan. A good metric should be understandable, comparable, and adaptable. It should best be expressed in percentages than absolute numbers; in that way, it is easier to review and compare for proper decision making. A good metric should be suited to your business type and your Lean business model. We made an earlier example of a business using the churn metric. From what we know about metrics and business stages, we can say that the company in question must be within stages two and three; Stickiness and Virality.

This is because these two stages are centered on customer feedbacks and customer retention, respectively. Now, this company is most likely to achieve great success because they realized the metric suiting to them at an immediate point and worked with it. This is where most start-ups get it wrong again. They sometimes do not know how to go about settling for the right metric for their business; they end up choosing the wrong ones. This is where hiring an experienced project manager would have been most beneficial, but in most cases of inexperience on the part of the project managers, the business just takes a deep dive into "no survival lane." Above all, a good metric should be adaptable; it should rise and shift as the business rises and shifts. The above-said company certainly cannot remain at "Churn" forever. The business advances, the metric should too. If the metric is moving and you do not know "for what," then it is not a good metric. This is necessary for comparison. You should be able to answer the questions consequently; "How was your metric the previous month or year?" "Is your conversation rate increasing?"

The proper study of the Lean Analytics metrics would give you an insight on which one is most suited for your business. In as much as a start-up should not necessarily try out everything that worked for others for themselves, rigidity is also not advisable. What do I mean by this? You should know when you come across a strategy with prospects, of course, after weighing the pros and cons and doing your necessary research and study. A start-up should be willing to change things for such strategies.

Various lean strategies are employable. It would be suicidal to limit yourself to one strategy alone or the same old strategies hoping to drive and thrive on that for all time. A start-up adopting the Lean method should be of necessity, adaptable, open to fresh ideas and thoughts. It is Adaptability that got you into adopting the Lean strategy in the first place in contrast to the old conventional methodologies in existence in the business world today. You wanted something different! Do not shut your heart out to difference now. Keep the spirit alive! I know what I am talking about.

*Being Overly Data-driven: This is one of the dangers that are inherent in using the Lean methods that start-ups usually fall prey to. It can be said that the Lean Analytics method is quite data-driven, if not entirely. People consider it a big risk with the argument that using data to optimize one part of your business, without stepping back and looking at the big picture can be dangerous, if not fatal. This is true to some extent. Suggestions have risen that rather than being slaves to data, Lean methods should be used as just a tool. Data is a potent tool that can be very addictive, causing us to analyze everything. But like humans, the truth remains that a bulk of what we do is mostly unconscious and intuitive, based on past experiences and occurrences. This is where experience would play a huge role. Just the same way we do not need to run tests and experiments to know what to eat every day, or when to brush our teeth or what to wear, human judgment should be placed in balance to Lean methods. In as much as we try to follow informative data and set up structures to achieve results, we are not robots. We should rely on our intuitive, innovative unconscious sides for a split second while having the bigger picture in mind. The Lean methods are not restrictive. This is where some start-ups get it wrong again. It takes a level of experience and knowledge to know when to push the pause button on data and analysis and work some intuitive magic! Most start-ups, with their very rigid bosses or project managers, just follow it all from the books. They are slaves to data; at all times, allowing the data and information on the machinery tell them what to do. And then they ask, probably after the first few years, "Why does it still seem like we're missing out something?" Because you are! Just that little switch is what you need.

The big deal about start-ups is not really getting it started. Do not get me wrong; that is so much of a big deal! But then, beyond getting it started and running, there is the place of sustenance and growth. A start-up is never built with the intention of having it stay a start-up for all time to come. Certainly not! Every big business or establishment started from the start-up level, too; there is always a beginning. They ended up being pointers to other start-ups on where they want to see themselves in years to come. This is the vision behind every start-up, growth, and advancement. But do all achieve this? It cannot be all! Why did we take the pain of highlighting these mistakes and scrawny loopholes? Not because we wanted to show off brain capacities or wealth of knowledge, but because we are fans of advancing start-ups. We are the good guys; we have your best interests at heart. The deal is not for you to read this book like you would a novel, discarding it alongside its information in "someday isle." The deal is for you to take action. Having known what might seemingly be the factor responsible for the stunt in the growth of your start-up, make some changes, and try new methods.

Do a total re-evaluation. Get the waste out before it weighs down your start-up. What if you lack passion or love for what you do, and you have already come so far, then you can employ self-discipline. Find out the fresh sides of what you do, what makes it essential, and the weight of its value, you will begin to grow some love. Make yourself realize that it is something worth doing. Employ staff who love it obviously more than you would ever do. Even when you think of giving up, they keep pushing and seeing them push, believe it or not, give you a level of strength to push a bit further. And if you ate just about to launch your start-up of you have been brewing thoughts on starting one, then this material came to you in time, very handy! Do not fall prey to the standard errors highlighted in this book. For some start-ups, the consequence was fatal; they never got back on their feet. Do not let the same be your start-up story; take the right steps today!

Easy things/ways to be more effective with Lean

Have you ever tried to use a chainsaw to cut through grasses that are not as tall as your ankle? How effective would that be? There is a quote that says "if the purpose of a thing is not known, the misuse is inevitable" that's true. When you don't properly understand how to use a chainsaw, you might use on grasses that aren't as tall as your ankle.

Lean is from the Japanese word "Muda" which means waste, which means that lean is more waste-reducing oriented. It optimizes the process of manufacturing a product to generate maximum value from the process with minimum input and the best customer experience.

Lean is a very effective tool if you know how to use it; in this case, knowledge is power and this power can change your business. Here are easy things to do with Lean to improve success in your business.

Get your staff trained: we talked about this in the previous; but it is one of the ways to be successful with lean. Like the analogy we gave earlier, you need to be sure that a bicycle should not be ridden indoors unless you have enough space to contain it. Your staff needs to know what the process is all about before you introduce it to the organization. Take out some months, and get them conversant with how Lean works sigma works. Let them get conversant with the Lean principles which are;

Value: this is defined by the recipient/customer/client. They define what they want to get out of the product, not the other way round. That means you would be listening attentively to what your customer defines value as—demand determines supply.

Value stream: how this value is produced without waste is the focus of lean. You must learn how to design this value with the minimum input and the maximum output.

Flow: you need to design processes that ensure maximum value production. The entire work process would be redefined to suit this.

Pull: after designing, test to see if customers would pull value from the product. You have to be sure.

Perfection: test again, and again until you are sure the product meets the client standard. You don't want to push a product out there and into the market and have customers complained because of details that were missed.

People centered: every lean process respects people. Even though the entire process is designed to meet the consumer's needs, it does not neglect the staff. The staff is a very important piece to this whole mix; without their input, there won't be any product. Respect for staff is encouraged. You would raise an empathetic team.

They also have to have an idea of what benefits lean comes with; waste elimination, less stress on the workforce, reduced cost, process flows optimally, improves lead time, product quality is affected, information is easily disseminated.

Breathe the air others breathe: after you get your staff trained, you would want to see the impact of this method on other businesses. You might want to take a tour around and see organizations that employ lean and those that don't. Note the difference. Experience, as we all know, is the best teacher they say, but it doesn't have to be your experience. You can learn better from what others have experienced. So take a tour, ask the best questions. The power of questioning is the best way to root-cause-analyze. That means if you want to find solutions quickly; you need to ask the best questions quickly. The question determines the answer. You must also understand that not everything that works for you, would work for others. That means, you have to use these general principles to formulate your own method; it's like skincare products, they all have a unifying factor; a principle that brings them all together, but they function differently. The processes you might need to adjust in your own organization might not be ones that another organization needs to reorganize. Just learn what you can and go on. Let their success motivate you and their mistakes inspire you. You might read about it, but nothing stands in the way of experiencing the implementation first hand, you would see how these organizations use the lean tools to maneuver real-life situations.

You would need to improve your own strategy: imagine that you wanted to build a sky scrapper and you had no architectural plan, you might go on and on about how beautiful the building would look and how strong it would be and the storms that it can resist; all that motivation might well be useless because you do not have a solid plan to work with. Plans should be realistic and feasible. The lean methodology would be woven around your plans and nothing else. It means if you don't have a plan, you might as well just close down the organization because lean methodology would not be effective. You should have a strategy that your entire team can look back to and work with so that implementing lean would be easier and smoother—there would be a solid foundation to build the entire process on.

Try labeling: as crude as this sounds, this is the foundation of organizing; people need to work, people also need tools to work with, let us save ourselves the stress of looking for tools and equipment that we could have easily found if they were labeled properly. Whether they are virtual tools/files or not, labeling or tagging them properly helps your team to easily navigate through to find what they need. It saves time and it makes work more efficient.

Set short term goals: short term goals come with their own motivation and energy. They also streamline the big, overall goal into small bits that can be worked on little by little until the ultimate goal is achieved and the company progresses. Goals without timeframes might at best be called wishes; time gives perspective to goals. If you say "we are going to expand our product penetration in the black populace" you need to really define what this means in clear terms, the strategy necessary to carry this out, and the time frame by which this should have been carried out and expired.

Let your results be visible: success is a motivator on its own. If you win a war right now, you would be motivated to win more. That's why games have levels so that you would not lose motivation at any point; the wins are designed to spur you to achieve more. You should have a culture of always showing results on your lean board; let your people see that progress is being made with all the investment you are making; the sight of progress and success motivates people to act.

Communicate: the reason why you might not benefit from the lean process would be because of poor communication; even though you might have a lean board, people might not have access to it. Communication is how the team is carried along; you need to carry your whole team along so that they can be effective. Each team needs to know what the other team is currently doing. This encourages team spirit and team commitment; they would look out for each other automatically because they know what is going on.

Don't be rigid: flexibility is the best way to lead because humans are complex and ever-changing. If change is a constant, flexibility must be your go to guy. You cannot be rigid on the way the process is expressed; you have to be on the lookout for bottlenecks and how to free them to allow ease and a better flow of work.

Bad processes would make a bad team: imagine having a monkey in a swimming pool, it could learn to swim eventually but it would not perform to its optimum. That's what bad processes are to people; they bring out the worst in them. If you begin to notice certain behavior in your team that as affected their effectiveness, immediately check out the process they are involved in, the process might be wrong for them. Lean gives you the opportunity to notice these flaws and checkmate them before they steal your queen.

Don't just plan, implement: if you just talk without carrying out, what good would the lean process be? Actions are what deliver results, not just plans. Plans are there to guide your actions to that you can achieve a certain goal, so don't just say it, do it and see how effective your organization would be.

Various Metrics to look out for in a Lean Business to ensure Business Productivity

What is Lean In business?

What is Lean?

Lean is a business method that's used to bring about improvement in manufacturing and to increase satisfaction for the customer while cutting down, in any way permissive, on wastes. Lean is about customer satisfaction through creating the customer kind of value and at the same time reducing such wastes as are provided during production. Wastes are those elements or processes that do not add anything to the creation of value and satisfaction of the customer.

Lean has one sole and core value or priority, and that is to satisfy the customer, to achieve this one goal, lean makes use of certain principles. Lean operates based on some core principles, these lean principles help keep the practice stayed on achieving one main thing, customer satisfaction. Briefly below are the lean core principles:

- Value definition: According to the Lean Methodology, value is whatever the customer is willing to pay for. This is not about what the company or organization thinks or assumes would be good for the customer or that the customer SHOULD buy. It's not about what the customer NEEDS, but what he or she WANTS. What people want is what they will go for, not what you think they need. So first it is expedient to understand this one rule for defining value according to Lean practices, it must be from the perspective of the customer, not yours.
- Value Stream Mapping (VSM): the next process and principle of Lean is what is known as the Value stream mapping, what this principle entails is that once the value is defined, that value is used as a landmark for improvement. Every activity or tool that is used in producing this value will now be checked, and those tools and activities that are not useful for the value to be created. These elements are referred to as *wastes,* and

they are divided into two categories; non-value but relevant, and non-valid and irrelevant. The second category will be completely removed because it is a complete waste, while the first category will be reduced. Through this means the customer ends up getting exactly what he or she wants while the company at the same time eliminates unnecessary activities and resources, this, in turn, reduces the cost of production and the cost of service.

- Flow: at the end of defining value and value stream mapping, it is important to ensure that there is a smooth flow of the production process since there has been some alteration through the removal of certain activities and items. This principle ensures that the flow of activities now is without interruptions and that it runs smoothly. In order to achieve this, there will be the need to reconfigure the production processes, break down the steps, and level out on the tasks. There may need to create a cross-functional sector while teaching the project workers to be flexible and highly competent so as to easily adapt and work with the new adjustments.

- Establishing Pull System: pull is a system that is created to ensure that new inventions are rightly managed and that the work in process (WIP) is limited. That is to say, only what is needed is produced. A pull system works through just-in-time service delivery and production. It requires that manufacturing takes place only when there is a need for it. On the other hand, deliveries come in time, there is no need for producing more products than is presently required, and they are usually produced and delivered right in time, and only the quantity required is as well produced. All these are done from the need of the customer.
- Perfection: While the first four principles are important, encouraging and ensuring that your employees and workers are excellent goes a long way to sustain improvement. Lean works in a continuous improvement scale, and how well anything is done after considering all four principles is dependent on the workforce. They must be competent.

These are the five lean principles through which its core value is achieved, customer satisfaction. For a business to be called or recognized as a lean business, it must follow the lean concepts, tools, and principles. The lean methodology upholds the respect for people and an unbroken chain of communication between workers and customers. Lean is flexible and allows for innovation, given that it greatly and ideally helps to satisfy the end customer's needs. Lean methodology encourages self-growth amongst workers as a way to work effectively and achieve perfection and excellence. In the end, the end customer gets exactly what he or she wants, how he or she wants it, and when he or she wants it.

A lean business:

A lean business is one that is interested in making continuous improvement and that through satisfying the customer. A lean business will adopt and operate on the culture of the lean methodology. In lean, it is about people, individual people instead of a group of market targets. Lean operates in a way that gives each customer what he or she wants. This does not negate the need sometimes to think about the whole target market, but lean basically are interested in knowing what each individual customer thinks of a product or a service. However, the possibility of meeting each customer's needs is dependent on the system of the business and their flexibility and willingness to adopt new styles that will allow them to meet the needs of each individual customer.

A Lean business does not operate a rigid documented system, where innovation is not allowed. Rather, it empowers its workforce to be creative and competent. Lean teaches its workforce to learn how to do stuff by themselves other than telling them how to do them all the time. Lean gives room for each person to suggest their opinion and ways they think improvement can be obtained in the company. This encourages their problem-solving skills to be sharpened, and gives them a sense of responsibility and compels then to strive to be better at what they do. In this case, business or company managers maintain a close association with their team of workers and that aids in attaining their goal.

WHAT ARE METRICS?

Metrics are calculative measures that are used for the purpose of tracking and reviewing the state of your business, and performances. It is how you determine whether or not your business is doing well. Different persons are involved in a business, so whatever the metric, they must address the workforce and the customers, the investors and the managers. Every aspect of a business has a specific performance metrics to it, but generally, metrics are those quantifying measures with which you keep the status and performance of your business in check.

Lean helps your business grow and improve continuously, business metrics, on the other hand, helps you follow up on the growth and performance of your business. It helps determine how much or how well your business is doing with all the lean principles and practices in having been put in place. Take for example, in marketing, marketers have a metric system to with which and through which they stay on the success of their marketing, the same thing applies to media advertisers and as well for politicians who do campaigns. In the cause of this, there are questions that will be asked, questions such as how many persons were we able to reach, and how many persons responded, and then how many persons gave a positive response? The idea is to know what the success and the failure is, having a target result in mind with which they will judge the performance result.

A metric is more like a guide; it helps your business track and achieves target results. In that case, there are certain checkpoints or tracking measures. Let us take an athlete for example; they know they train against various factors. They have to train enough to get to the point where they can now beat the time. Time is probably the athlete's highest target. This is how a metric works:

Emily is an athlete, and she swims. There's a competition coming up and in order for her to make it as a winner, she has to beat the time by half. The time is set for one minute in each swim to the end of the pool and back, and she has not been able to go beyond fifty seconds for the same task. Emily no longer has just time to beat, but every other factor that will aid her effort to beat the time by half, that is thirty seconds. For a swimmer, she will have to consider her factors in this order:

- Time
- Intervals
- Stroke count

- Heart rate
- Calories
- Stroke type

These are what make up the metrics for a swimmer, success or performance result for Emily would be very positive when she is able to beat the time by half since that is her target. She will be able to cover the interval within that time frame. Emily can decide to go on a weight-loss routine if watching her calorie intake can help her achieve her goal. Knowing what stroke type works best for her would also help her be able to navigate at every point. All these factors when they are properly managed will work together to ensure that Emily hits her target. Without this metric, Emily will not be able to train to beat the time. But because she has this metric and knows how to tackle each factor, she can get herself to the point she wants.

The more Emily practices and keeps going back to her metrics to weigh her performances, the better she gets at doing what she loves to do. It is not just athletes that follow up on their performance results so as to get better in what they do. There are people and organizations everywhere that follow certain structures as a way to track their progress and to get better.

The same applies to a business, there are factors to watch out for and follow as a marker to achieve performance target result. A business metric allows for an improvement in productivity, and while that goes on, it also helps to determine how much of that improvement is on-going.

A lean business would measure progress through the lens of the lean five principles and core value. A lean business would consider one major thing above every other possible factor, and that is customer satisfaction. Usually, feedback and reviews are topmost for companies and organizations to understand their customers and to track their own progress and performance.

For such businesses and organizations that are interested in creating a trustworthy service and delivering excellent values to the customer, they would also need to ensure that their flow is steady. In order to achieve this, they will need to have some kind of structure that watches the success of that flow and measure the end performance. This is the only way to spot out areas that can use some improvement and keep at it. The more the loopholes, the less show success, and they can now know that they need to put in more work or discover what they are not doing right or what they're not doing at all.

All in all, business metrics are those factors you look out for as a measuring tape to determine success in your business. Success determination can be measured by counting the positives or it can be done by counting the negatives. A business should have a measuring mark for progress and performance, just like the athlete Emily. If Emily couldn't beat the time target by half before the competition, she will most likely not win the competition.

The lean metrics increases the possibilities or improving in businesses or other organizations by pointing out and measuring the degree of waste and variations that lead to dissatisfaction of the customer. These metrics, when incorporated into a business or company, can help the business or organization achieve its goals.

NEED FOR METRICS

As someone who just started a business, you may doubt the need for certain things and just take them to be a total waste of time, you probably will liken it to buying a new item and reading its terms and conditions – nobody does that, or you may see it as a new gadget you just got from a store – who reads manuals anyway, unless you're an android user who now has an iPhone. Funny right? And yet the story is different when it comes to business, startups to be precise; you need every bit of information you can lay your hands on, no matter how trivial it may sound.

Take for instance John, John started a company from scratch, he had money, quite a lot and hated to be told what to spend his money on. John was tech-savvy and decided to grow a company, he hired some other persons and they got to work, his plan was to build an application software which would let you know when a neighbor has electricity in their house through any means; it could be via a generator set, solar panel, just whatever, so when there's no electricity in your house but there is nearby, you could simply walk up there and join in. John's target market was Africa, he knew some countries there had a severe power outage and majority of the businesses which thrive there depend solely on a generator set, he knew the problem won't be fixed any time soon, the issue may last over a decade, so he got to work with his team. In no time, the application software was ready and public announcements made (as money was not a problem). A day to the "big day", John's system was hacked, and the application software stolen. It was an "inside job" which would have been avoided if there were metrics put in place to automate responses to changes, build a holistic view of the environment and alert other human beings when required. The application software was revamped and released on a later date by former members of his team. He couldn't sue them because there was no evidence. Don't be like John, prioritize metrics!

Before plunging explicitly into the need for metrics and why it should be monitored, let's look at some misconceptions about it

1. Metrics are for measuring people – The false nature of this statement is overwhelming, this is totally wrong, metrics measures the contribution of the team, it is simply an organizational tool put

in place to foster efficiency on the paraphernalia in use and on the effectiveness of the team

2. You put metrics in place because you want to punish those that are guilty – Here goes another false statement. Metrics help solve problems and identify areas of opportunity, you don't use them to punish employees. With metrics in place, you know the exact problems to solve and you're not left to grope in the dark

3. Everything must be measured – It is better to keep things easy so that everyone understands what is going on, you don't pull out statistics which only the statistician and a few other employees understand perfectly and ask everyone to go to work on them, it would fail and, in the end, you will be blamed

4. Whatever you can't control, you can't measure – Measure what needs to be measured. In essence,

whatever it is your influence – that is what you can and should measure.

5. Very little data will go a long way – As William Thomson said "If you cannot measure it, you cannot improve it" whatever you don't measure cannot be managed, you must have clear objectives. You would never be able to tell if you are successful unless success is well-defined and monitored. The only way to achieve this in business is to quantify progress and adjust your process (mode of operation) to give you the desired result.

Metrics represent all raw measurements of resource usage or behavior which can be noted and gotten throughout systems, they tell you pertinent information about a process and give accurate measurements on how the process functions and they also provide a basis for suggestions for improvement.

Metrics are simply a standard or a system of measurement. In john's case (the example given above), inasmuch as there is a standard for measuring security, there should be specific standards set up for a particular company, which should be adjusted and fine-tuned to suit the needs of that company. If this was done, John wouldn't have found himself in that situation.

The need for having a metric system includes;

1. It will help drive the strategy and direction of the organization: When metrics are put in place, the path to take towards the organization's destination will be clearly known. For example, if the target of an organization is to reduce customer complaints to two per month than have a 40% reduction, all that is needed is a tweak to the metric and with proper communication with the employee, it will be achieved.

2. Focus: it will help put the organization, employees, and everyone involved in check and keep them constantly focused, with their eyes on the ball. If there is a target to meet in a month,

with the right metrics, the numbers will be rolled up so that progress can be tracked

3. Decision – In cases where decisions on certain matters need to be made, metrics are the best resort to turn to. It will help give out in clear terms, the need to make or not to make a move at a point

4. Performance – It enables an organization to do better. Metrics monitor activities going on, when this is viewed by the head of an organization, the level of progress made is known and the organization knows how much effort should be put in

5. Change and evolve with the organization – As metrics are being monitored, the organization changes and evolves as more progress is made, there is also an evolving of metrics as the organization strives to get better

6. Objective process – The goal of every organization is to make a profit and at the same time satisfy the customers, in a bid to satisfy customers, quality services must be rendered, processes have to be organized to suit the customer's needs. Metrics help transmogrify the bland requirements a customer gives into a series of numbers which can be used to distinctively map out the process for its efficiency. Metrics let us know if a process is good enough to meet the customer's needs or if it should be better.

WHAT ARE THE METRICS THAT YOU LOOK AT TO KNOW THAT LEAN IS AFFECTING THE HEALTH OF YOUR ORGANISATION?

Success must be measurable; if not, you cannot tell whether this is a success or not. To know if you are successful, you would first have to have a clearly defined perspective/vision. What did you want to achieve with this business you started? Where do you see this business in 50 years' time? All these are essential steps to know if one is along the path of success or not. With your vision in mind, you can quickly look at specific metrics to see if you are succeeding or not. Let's take a look at some of these KPI/metrics that prove the health of your organization and how close it is to its goal.

1. The cost that it would take to retain a customer: as a business, you should have a strategy that you implement to maintain customers, and that strategy is going to come with a cost, that cost should be minimal as you engage in lean methodologies; you should find more cost-effective ways to keep your customers. If you follow the number of consumers that engage your products monthly, the cost to design and deploy those products, how long those products last before they get purchased, the price of marketing, and maintenance, you can quickly figure out the cost of keeping your customer.
2. How viral is your product? The virality of your merchandise can be an excellent pointer to the health of your business. If you get more people to know you exist, you stand a better chance of

getting engaged. Your viral reach can be measured by how many you have participated on Facebook, Instagram, and Twitter. One of the best platforms to easily reach your chosen demographic is social media; it is a platform that allows for 2/3 of the entire world's population to be in one place. That means with the right strategy; you can easily reach a good number of prospective customers. If you can engage more people, you stand a better chance of scoring sales. By knowing your virality, you can understand how effective your product and your advertising strategy are.

3. There is something called "turnover" it is the number of customers or staff that have left or stop patronizing you. You can use lean methods to monitor this change. It is usual for people to leave an organization, but there is a rate at which people leave that indicates beyond any reasonable doubt that is abnormal. When you notice this, you quickly investigate the reason why you are having a considerable turnover or churn out rate; maybe it is the increase in price, or customer service, or poor HR policies, it could be anything. The drill is,

if you find something of that sort that raises any brows, look into it.

4. Every private sector organization is run by profit, and the public sector is run by the tax; they all fall into the bracket of REVENUE. Revenue is a perfect place to start if you want to measure the health of your business. It is the most logical thing to do. If you want to know if a company is going to survive or not, look at their revenue. The revenue is how much comes into a business after each sale; it goes beyond the profit that was made after sales; profit is the total amount of money that is left after you take out your expenditure and cost. Revenue, on the other hand, is the total amount of money that comes into an organization. There is a temptation to spend more because you are making more; if you have more revenue, it still doesn't mean that you cannot look for better ways to produce a product at a lesser cost?

5. Lead time: the lead time is the amount of time it takes for a product to go through a lean process to completion. To be able to track your progress, you definitely need to know how fast your

products are produced and how fast they get to the consumer. One thing you do not want to have on your sleeves is an unsatisfied customer giving a bad review on your product. One of the fastest ways to land a business engagement is through word of mouth, aka, referrals. Referrals are easily the quickest way to ensconce customer loyalty to your brand. If you want to get customers to buy from you, get someone they trust to speak about your product, and they would consider it. The faster the product delivery, the better reviews you would get. To make work more comfortable, you can design a reasonable lead timetable to help your customers know how long a particular product would take. Let me give you a sneak-peak into something; before you develop a lean time, check with your competitors to know what their lean time is so that you do not fix the time and discover that you are slower than your competitors.

6. How easily is work distributed among the team? This question is fundamental. It answers the issue of the workflow. For a product to reach its final stage, it goes through many departments, and

the rate at which this work gets executed is essential. Your company is healthy if your team members distribute well, have a strong team spirit, and deliver the task before or right on schedule.

7. Increased number of open issues: it is only reasonable that mistakes would be made, and problems would arise, but if these issues are becoming overwhelming, then it is imperative you look into it before it ruins something. The state of work is essential for the quality of the product—it is garbage in, garbage out. What you invest in, would, in turn, affect you.

8. Customer feedback: apart from internal evaluation, some external assessment is necessary as well. What your customer says about your product is the brand your product has in the mind of that customer. Branding is the unique identity that people encounter to understand what your business would do for them; if you ruin this by lousy service, it will affect ROI. Feedback is vital for the success of your business, and you need to be cautious of the kind of feedback you want to get from customers.

Do you want good feedback? Then give quality work.

What are the advantages of metrics?

Well, read John's story again. As we all know, you're in business first to make profit, when this fails to come to fruition or is just taking some time (even though you envisaged it) you become worried, angry at yourself and may decide to quit. It is important to note that the importance of metrics cannot be overemphasized.

Metrics give you an edge over seeming minute occurrences which may render your company bankrupt.

To get the best out of metrics, here are some guidelines and also some advantages

- Follow the steps: Metrics have lots of advantage but first you must follow the steps, you must know first consider what data to track. Selecting the right metrics involves some processes which include

  i.   *Define your business's governing objectives*; it is often said that "when the use of a thing is not known, abuse is inevitable". To be able to accurately know what to track, your objectives must be clearly defined, without this you would just keep going in circles and this could be very frustrating. It would look as though you are putting in so much work and having so little progress.

ii.	*Know what drives your business success*; you must come to an understanding of what enables you to make progress and turn out successful because this will determine what you should put more effort into. For some companies, it is the customers, this means they must provide quality services and have an outstanding marketer-customer relationship; this will improve feedback coming from the customers, which is good for business.

iii.	*What can the employees do to meet the governing objectives;* After the objectives have been outlined, it is very important to outline the things each employee can do to meet these objectives, if these are outlined specifically for each employee, it will reduce the case scenario where the employee doesn't know the job description i.e. the employee doesn't know what should be done at a given time

iv. *Statistics re-evaluation*; Regularly, statistics should be re-evaluated to check if the governing objectives are congruent with the activities of the employee, it could be re-evaluated every month or every 2 weeks to be sure the right activities are being carried out.

- Causality and convenience: when causality can be proven beyond doubt and when it can be accessed with ease for progress to be tracked between the employers and employees, it serves as an advantage. Once the analysis isolates critical variables for success, everything is in place and is perfect. If the effect of a certain marketing effort is what needs to be measured, isolate and unravel how those products influence the bottom line as compared to your regular approach. If same-product sales are a predictor of revenue growth, be sure to implement it. A dashboard approach is used most times for tracking purposes; it gives an instant look at the numbers which "call the shots" – this method is preferable as it alleviates you off the stress of having to go through a large report or a certain complicated spreadsheet repeatedly. If this approach will be taken, be sure to align your business and its goals to suit what is expected, a one-size-fits-all would not suffice for your business in this case as certain errors could be encountered and this is bad for business

- Choose carefully; Once you're able to choose carefully, the advantages abound; employees and resources will be pulled towards objectives which will grow business and measures to be chased will reflect company goals, employee compensation will not take over and numbers will no longer be the focus because metrics will reflect the exact state of the business, if it is faring well or not and not how well employees can guess what is being searched for hence they won't be able to manipulate the data to suit themselves. For example, a salesperson, who has an idea that judgments are made on yearly volumes may decide to place orders a day before the reporting period with prior knowledge that it will be canceled or returned later just so he can boost numbers. This will not occur because metrics will reflect exactly the exact state at which business is

- Data should decide; Metrics will be used to your advantage if it has the greatest utility for your business. Metrics will not exist and then you place your "knowledge" over it, you must let data decide. For example, you may think the number of people logging onto your website equates to the amount of money you get in a day. If metrics doesn't prove it as such, then it is not so and will never be. If metrics are in place, it should be the marker for growth and progress in your business, this way you will maximize profit and avoid unnecessary stress

- Not spend time and money on the wrong things; Once you focus on the right things, you take your hands off other stressful and unimportant things. This is made achievable with metrics, it gives you an easy way out

- Helps prioritize your tasks; you no longer lack priority like doing the unimportant but urgent things, metrics help you prioritize accurately and effortlessly. With metrics, you know exactly what to do to get the best results

What happens when you toss metrics away?

We all know too well that whatever has an advantage also has a disadvantage; the goal is in determining which one outweighs the other. Water is essential for growth in the human body, it is also essential to meet the daily needs of man, I mean, we all need to have our bath, wash clothes, cook, etc. When there is a flood, that's still water but this time around it will have a devastating effect on those who will get affected. Houses could be torn to shreds, river banks would overflow, etc., this doesn't mean water is bad; it is having the right quantity that matters. The same can be said also for metrics; can they be used to an advantage? Yes, can they also have some disadvantages? Yes.

There are different types of metrics, all of which employ numbers and economic principles to explain business performance. All business metrics have setbacks anyway, if not in the way they are designed, then it could be in how analysts can misuse them thereby producing incorrect results.

The disadvantages of metrics include but are not limited to;

1. Specificity: The high degree of specificity in which certain business metrics set up can be a

disadvantage. The use of data on security to create a result may be useful in learning about a sector of the business and likely ignores others, relegating them to the background hence they are seen as unimportant. For example, the market position reveals how much of a given market a certain business controls through its sales. As a gauge or marker of general stability, however, this is a poor metric analysis since it doesn't tell about the growth potential of the market or whether a business competes in several markets at the same time. Focusing a lot of effort on one facet could lead to other components being ignored and this will be terrible for business

2. Inaccuracy: The goal of business metrics is to break down complex realities in different facets of an organization's existence into minute chunks of data which can be easily comprehended, recorded and compared with former or subsequent data. Some metrics, however, include the risk of inaccuracy, making them totally dangerous to use when there is money to be sought after or even

heightens doubt about results instead of them being doused. This majorly is the case with metrics that rely solely on forecasts or estimates. Predictions based on research and past results, could be the information originating from a company's static budget and may look like sound financial information; when actual data is finally inserted by analysts, there could be a humongous change in industry growth as a result of incorrect assumptions which have previously been made on areas including inflation, expenses, etc.

3. Over-reliance: The benchmarks for evaluating performance for some metrics such as profit-and-loss statements, the cash asset ratio could be overly relied upon and in the end be outrightly wrong. Inasmuch as these metrics have value, the illusion is also formed that other metrics amount to no good and are less reliable neither can they be trusted. The responsibility of evaluating business metrics within the context of what those metrics represent are foisted exclusively on individuals, what other metrics reveal and how

information works in sync to give information about a business are also subject to what individuals make of them.

4. Wrong numbers: When metrics are used improperly and not in line with your objectives or won't have the desired effect on the bottom line, it would be a disadvantage. Metrics need to be predictive and persistent for them to be useful and a regular comparison of the statistic measures to the desired outcome. If massive importance is placed on metrics which do not guarantee any progress as regards your strategic objectives and the mission of your organization, it means you're going the wrong way.

If you also measure events which occur out of sheer luck and consider them to be benchmarks for success in the future, you're slowly running into error and will fall sooner or later – a man who stays in an area where the weather is pretty cool around September and his sale of umbrellas are fair and in the month of March which is hottest, there is a political campaign and the party involved use umbrellas as a campaign strategy, it would be wrong for him to outrightly equate his massive sale of umbrellas in march to the political campaign, ignoring the weather, for he would only later realize it was less effective than planned and the metric put in place was useless.

5. Easy to manipulate: If your metrics can easily be manipulated, it would be a disadvantage to the growth of your business. If your employees find out that as a radio presenter, your main goal is to gain listeners, they may just get friends to write down fake names, sign up and eventually unsubscribe almost immediately. It is pertinent to look for metrics that are safest and will not be manipulated. A superficial metric is no man's friend

6. Contrasting goals: When your interest is not taken to heart and your employees careless, they would do the opposite, and a negative outcome will ensue. Once the interest of the employer differs

from that of the employee, clashes are imminent. If an employee is judged based on the number of goods sold, he might try to game the system by hiring "customers" to come buy so that he will be duly compensated, as they return the goods sooner or later.

7. You are not your metrics: it is quintessential that you don't get caught in the web of assuming you are your metrics. You are the first human, business involves lots of highs and lows, and sometimes you could be at the lows. While it is important to track your metrics, never tie your value to numbers because it will destroy you emotionally. When metrics don't look good, as humans, we think and feel, this could lead to uncoordinated acts on the part of the individuals involved.

8. Human factors: Metrics could make you ignore human factors and all you do is stay focused on numbers. If human factors are responsible for a

dip in business, there's no need focusing on numbers, the human factors should be fixed, are the employees happy, do they get enough rest, are they burning out? Human factors are as important as data and numbers, do not get one at the expense of the other

9. Vanity metrics: These include metrics like social media attention, shares, and page views. While these have no role to play in your bottom line, they could make you feel good, who doesn't need a little boost from something like that anyway, the morale it gives could be a boost to the team. Focusing excessively on metrics will take this away. Learn to enjoy the little "pointless" numbers.

Conclusion

You have the knowledge, you have the incentive, and you even have the support to create your own start-up. What else is needed? The right kind of analytics, of course! It doesn't matter how smart, motivated or ambitious an entrepreneur is he must always remember the fatalistic mistake to create what no one needs. By studying the rules for using lean analytics to measure your business operations, you are guaranteed to learn how to develop your start-up in the right direction.

So, what are the main points that you need to analyse in a start-up? And how can you apply this analysis to your company's growth? These are the few questions that Lean Analytics answers.

The beauty with lean analytics and the lean method in general is that the end goal is not success or failure per project. Rather, the end goal is an iterative improvement per project. So, whether a business model succeeds or fails is not much of a concern to the lean entrepreneur. Rather, the bother is on what can be improved upon with each new project, product or service.

What is the main idea communicated in this book and with it the methodology?

If you describe in two sentences, you get the following:

At each stage of start-up development there is only one project metric that is most important at the moment and it is the measurement and change of this metric that leads to the success of the entire project. This "magic" metric should have predetermined critical values, on the basis of which certain managerial decisions are prescribed in advance.

What should be a priority for you?

Start-up founders should study and analyse metrics, not depend on them

What is a start-up? This is an organization aimed at creating a sustainable and reproducible business model. Perhaps you have already thought about creating your own business?

If so, then you should have all the necessary information for the development of your business and the ability to soberly assess your capabilities.

What are metrics?

This is numerical information vital to your business. If you, for example, launch a media site, then you need data on the number of advertising if you are an investor, then you need to know all the parameters of return on investment.

One of the reasons metrics are important is that entrepreneurs often lie a little to themselves when evaluating their success. In the end, numerical information is needed to convince other people (such as investors) that your idea will work.

In any case, if you dream too much, then your start-up probably will not survive. You must rely on the real capabilities of your business to be successful - for this you need metrics.

Metrics are an antidote to self-deception. Allowing you to soberly evaluate your success, they keep you on the right track: based on these metrics, you will see a clear picture of the development of your start-up.

However, you should not become a robot focused on numbers only. Your personal opinion is also very important! Do not let metrics take precedence when making decisions. It is enough to take into account your own parameters, but not to put them "at the forefront".

Metrics are undoubtedly an important parameter for analysis, but do not get used to them: you run the risk of getting into a difficult situation using metrics to optimize your business, because numerical data is only one facet of business development.

Ultimately, your metrics must lead you to the right product and the right market, before your money runs out. But you must also find an effective way to evaluate your success. This means that you must choose the analysis method that will lead you to relevant and relevant information.

A good analyst has three important characteristics: it has comparisons, is understandable, and is also most effective as a key factor.

Comparative analytics shows the development process. You must compare different metrics: day, week, morning, day, evening etc., consumer groups, and competitor metrics. The phrase "increased revenue last week," for example, says a lot more than just "2 percent of revenue."

Good analytics should also be understood. The indicators of your metrics should help you make decisions about what to do in a particular situation, and what development strategy should be chosen as a whole, but if no one can understand or remember these indicators, then they are useless. This will not lead to any positive changes in your organization. Therefore, use available analytics concepts, such as "weekly revenue."

But the most useful metric indicators are coefficients (proportions).

Firstly, it's easier to work with coefficients. For example, if you are launching a media site, you need information about the number of "advertising clicks". Daily information on this indicator is certainly important, however, it is much more useful to know if you have reached the planned number of visitors. This will help you understand what should be optimized in your strategy.

Secondly, the coefficients are comparable in nature. They allow you to compare short-term and long-term metrics: "The number of clicks from advertisements per month," for example, this is one of the metrics, and the ratio of the number of daily visitors to the average number of visitors during the month will allow you to judge the growth in site popularity or vice versa.

Founders of start-ups should concentrate on what they are good at and on how their favourite business can bring income

The success of a start-up directly depends on what the demand for its product and the desire of the founder to help ensure that demand and supply overlap.

To get started, find what you are really interested in. Creating a start-up is not just creating a product and promoting it. Ask yourself: what do you really want to create

Do not start a business that you will hate, because if you are not happy with what you are doing, then for sure it will not be successful. In addition, investors tend to look for founders who are truly passionate about solving a particular problem. You will not attract investment if you lack enthusiasm and are removed from business.

Secondly, make sure that you are really good at something. If you define your niche in the market, then you will understand that not one who will try to fill it. You must meet customer needs better than your competitors.

And remember: never start businesses where everyone can compete with you equally. You need a kind of advantage, for example a group of friends and contacts who will help improve your chances of success.

Lastly, make sure that you can make money by doing what you want. In the end, this is what the business starts for: encourage people to pay you for what you do.

www.ingramcontent.com/pod-product-compliance
Lightning Source LLC
Chambersburg PA
CBHW070338220526
45467CB00001B/156